Literature in Perspective

General Editor: Kenneth H. Grose

Mediæval Drama

Literature in Perspective

Mediæval Drama

A. M. Kinghorn

Evans Brothers Limited, London

Published by Evans Brothers Limited
Montague House, Russell Square, London, W.C.1
© A. M. Kinghorn 1968
First published 1968

Set in 11 on 12 point Bembo and printed in Great Britain by
The Camelot Press Ltd., London and Southampton
237 35065 3 Cased   PR4373
237 35066 1 Limp

Literature in Perspective

Of recent years, the ordinary man who reads for pleasure has been gradually excluded from that great debate in which every intelligent reader of the classics takes part. There are two reasons for this: first, so much criticism floods from the world's presses that no one but a scholar living entirely among books can hope to read it all; and second, the critics and analysts, mostly academics, use a language that only their fellows in the same discipline can understand.

Consequently criticism, which should be as 'inevitable as breathing'—an activity for which we are all qualified—has become the private field of a few warring factions who shout their unintelligible battle cries to each other but make little communication to the common man.

Literature in Perspective aims at giving a straightforward account of literature and of writers—straightforward both in content and in language. Critical jargon is as far as possible avoided; any terms that must be used are explained simply; and the constant preoccupation of the authors of the Series is to be lucid.

It is our hope that each book will be easily understood, that it will adequately describe its subject without pretentiousness, so that the intelligent reader who wants to know about Donne or Keats or Shakespeare will find enough in it to bring him up to date on critical estimates.

Even those who are well read, we believe, can benefit from a lucid exposition of what they may have taken for granted, and perhaps—dare it be said?—not fully understood.

K. H. G

Mediæval Drama

Mediæval drama is religious drama, a new birth, conceived within the Roman Church liturgy but drawing away from it to form an independent growth. In order to furnish the faithful with Christian instruction and entertainment outside the regular offices of the Church the composers of Latin and French vernacular plays drew upon a complex religious heritage. *Ludus Danielis*, an ecclesiastical ancestor of opera, and *Le Mystère d'Adam*, a popular play, both conceived in the 12th century, differ widely in character but both may claim descent from the Easter Trope or 'Quem Quaeritis'.

In England the outstanding dramatic development was the Corpus Christi Cycle, first staged in Chaucer's time and performed in the streets of English towns until the last quarter of the 16th century. The young Shakespeare must have witnessed late performances of these miracle plays and his own works were profoundly affected by them. Moralities, which clothed the doctrines of the preachers with life, and interludes, dealing with a diversity of subject-matter, both gave playwrights opportunity to develop their own plots, peopled by vital characters such as one might have encountered in contemporary England. *The Castell of Perseverance*, *Everyman*, and *Magnyfycence* mark stages in the movement towards freedom of invention, but the Tudor comedies *Ralph Roister Doister* and *Gammer Gurton's Needle*, together with the tragedy *Gorboduc*, although written under the influence of the classical dramatists Plautus, Terence and Seneca, nevertheless owe a great deal to the power of mediæval acting traditions. Plays like *Dr. Faustus*, *Measure For Measure*, *Hamlet*,

7

and *Every Man in His Humour* show many signs of the working-out of this power.

The author takes this opportunity to record and acknowledge his debt to Mr. K. H. Grose for his wise editing and to two colleagues in the sunswept Caribbean, Mr. C. S. Jackson and Dr. G. Büscher, for their constructive comments on Chapter 2. Thanks are due, also, to those pupils whose tutorial *aperçus* did not pass unnoticed, and to Mrs. M. Warren for her extremely efficient work on the typescript.

A. M. K.

Contents

The Author

A. M. Kinghorn, M.A., Ph.D., is Reader in English Literature in the University of the West Indies, Jamaica.

Acknowledgements

The author and publishers are indebted to the following for permission to use illustrations: the Trustees of the British Museum for the miniature of mediæval musicians and the page of manuscript from the York Cycle, and the Universitäts-Bibliothek, Freiburg, for the scene from a mediæval picture-bible.

Our thanks are also due to Oxford University Press, Inc., for permission to reproduce the music on page 34, which is taken from *The Play of Daniel* (© 1959).

I

The Nature of Drama

Drama is a Greek word, meaning *action*, or *something done*. It was used by the Greeks in its more limited sense of 'stage play'; Aristophanes in *The Frogs* employs it in this way when he makes Euripides say 'the play goes on', referring to a performance by actors impersonating an action within the compass of natural experience, but as a *performance* distinguishable from real life. Nowadays we think of drama as 'dramatic', that is, exciting, full of movement and spectacle, and we talk about 'dramatic art', referring to performances on a stage for the emotional and intellectual pleasure of an audience. When we go to the theatre we expect action on the stage, and we also hope not to be bored by a lack of excitement or movement; we want our play to be fairly close to real life, with characters whom we can recognise as having a 'psychology' like our own, who will entertain us, interpret experience and convey ideas and information which we did not have before. One important ingredient of the conventional stage play is speech—whether it is the grandiloquence of Romeo's overblown metaphors:

> It was the lark, the herald of the morn,
> No nightingale: look, love, what envious streaks
> Do lace the severing clouds in yonder east:
> Night's candles are burnt out, and jocund day
> Stands tiptoe on the misty mountain tops:
> I must be gone and live, or stay and die.

to which Juliet, reluctant to part with her lover, replies:

> Yon light is not daylight, I know it, I:
> It is some meteor that the sun exhales,

> To be to thee this night a torch-bearer,
> And light thee on thy way to Mantua:
> Therefore stay yet; thou need'st not to be gone.

ROMEO AND JULIET III, 5, 6–16

or the more ambiguous dialogue between Thomas à Becket and the Fourth Tempter in *Murder in the Cathedral*:

Thomas: Who are you? I expected
          Three visitors, not four.
Tempter: Do not be surprised to receive one more,
          Had I been expected, I had been here before.
          I always precede expectation.
Thomas: Who are you?
Tempter: As you do not know me, I do not need a name,
          And, as you know me, that is why I come.
          You know me, but have never seen my face.
          To meet before was never time or place.

Part I, 476–85

or the exchange between Abraham and Isaac when the boy is just beginning to realise that there is something strange about his father's behaviour before the sacrifice. Isaac asks:

> Father, yf yt be your will,
> Wher is the beaste that we shall kill?

and Abraham answers:

> Therof, sone, is non upon this hill,
> That I see here in this steade.

whereupon Isaac, afraid that he himself is to be the victim, says:

> Father, I am full sore affearde
> To see you beare that drawne swerde:
> I hope for all myddel-earde
>   You will not slaye your childe.

THE SACRIFICE OF ISAAC, CHESTER CYCLE

All these represent varying degrees of sophistication in dialogue, and reveal the kind of mental action going on in the play as well as the nature of the relationship between the speakers, to mention but two of the more obvious lines of communication suggested by these examples. Yet speech is not a necessary ingredient of play-acting, and *charade*, in fact, fulfils all its basic requirements. This is particularly obvious in silent films, when the mime of a Chaplin or a Buster Keaton is in itself sufficient to make the audience laugh, without the embellishment of deliberately-timed cross-talk. A play which derives most of its interest from what its characters say and lacks physical movement may be less 'dramatic', but since Marlowe wrote *Tamburlaine* English drama has developed linguistic sophistication to such an extent as to compel playwrights to depend for communication upon the resources of the language rather than upon visual effects. This kind of play has come to be called 'poetic' drama, though this description does not necessarily exclude prose; the prose-plays of Ibsen, for example, are often highly poetic, while one could mention numerous verse-plays of which this is not true.

We have already taken one illustration from *Romeo and Juliet*. This is a play, written in the last decade of the 16th century, about a young man and woman whose families are at enmity, whose love for each other is so powerful as to inspire them to defy the feuding groups, who get married but are overtaken by their families' quarrel and die in what may prosaically be called 'tragic' circumstances. The plot concerns the human condition and deals with experiences which have been known to touch European society. As summarised above, it may seem superficial and not particularly outstanding; the story might make up the substance of a popular novel, and Shakespeare borrowed the skeleton from a poem by Arthur Brooke called *The Tragicall History of Romeus and Juliet* (1562). Brooke himself took the story from a French translation of an Italian collection of tales by Bandello, printed in 1554, but the Romeo and Juliet romance goes back at least a century before that. Shakespeare's poetic imagination transformed the old narrative into a powerful revelation of a pattern of human experience by penetrating beneath the surface of the action and finding there certain basic themes, 'birth and copulation and death', which together with destiny are controlling forces in our lives. The lovers are fated to meet, fall in love and die under the cloud of family vendetta; it is this inter-relationship of personal circumstances with destiny which binds Romeo to Juliet in life and in death, and makes the pair no longer one particular man and one particular woman but rather universal or 'archetypal' man and woman. We see ourselves in them, for, as Hamlet says, playing holds the mirror up to nature.

More difficult to comprehend is the level of dramatic communication at which the 'transcendent' or 'ideal' is expressed, and the only way in which this can be done convincingly is through symbols. At the end of *Romeo and Juliet*, the Montagues and the Capulets are reconciled, irretrievably bound by the two golden statues, the 'poor sacrifices of our enmity', which the elders of the two families resolve to erect as a material symbol of the terrible results of their traditional discord; but this is only a pointer to Shakespeare's symbol of reconciliation, an ineffable one, implicit in the final gathering of the threads. More obvious is the symbol of the mystical Duke in *Measure for Measure*, who is almost an incarnation of divinity, emerging as a figure of compassion and atonement. The Greek dramatists used to make this even clearer by making the god, or *deus ex machina*, take part in the action of the play itself and give form to the chaos created out of human failure and misunderstanding. T. S. Eliot is one modern playwright who follows this ritual method as, for example, in *The Family Reunion*, wherein the presence of the Eumenides or Fates is intended to be taken as a commentary on what has gone before, though many modern dramatists seek subtler and more suggestive ways of indicating a supernatural 'presence', so that the audience senses rather than sees or hears it. The last scene of *Hamlet* permits the introduction of a revitalising influence, which banishes the violence and terror of the action and leaves us curiously satisfied, even optimistic, about the future potential of man. All this is not quite like real life, and it is through the dramatist's special gift that we see on the stage actions, bolder, more extravagant, more concentrated and more deliberately contrived than those which we encounter in our humdrum lives. The best drama is life-enhancing, and holds our interest by concentrating only on essentials and avoiding dullness.

Nowadays, therefore, it is hardly possible to think of serious drama without accepting the fact that the foundation of a play is words, and that the action, the characterisation, the stagecraft, and even the costumes are all summed up in the spoken words prepared by the playwright for the producer, the actors, the designer and the audience to work upon. When these words affect us, they communicate his knowledge of meanings, such as the meaning of the sin of Oedipus, of Romeo's love for Juliet, the meaning of Macbeth's guilt or of Faust's pact with the Devil. Questions are implied, such as: Why does the just man often suffer when the villain gets off scot-free? Does crime, in fact, pay? Why are we tempted at the very moment when we cannot resist? Why do we, by choosing one good, sometimes destroy another? Why are good people often so troublesome to live with? Why is talent given no opportunity to reveal itself? Why does one choose what seems to be the lesser evil but which is in fact the greater? Why must the young be sacrificed for the old? Why is the light shown when the way is darkest? All these are questions suggested by individual plays of Shakespeare and the reader can perhaps work out for himself which plays these are. However, no explicit answers are given by Shakespeare to any of these moral problems, and we need not look for satisfaction in the plots themselves; the characters do not tell us plainly what they are trying to do, and what they say is full of half-hints, double-meanings, paradoxes and ambiguities. The dramatist's ordering of situation seems to solve puzzles and give his audience various degrees of emotional and intellectual pleasure.

MEDIÆVAL DRAMA

So far we have referred mainly to post-Renaissance drama, and our attention has been understandably drawn to Shakespeare and his successors, who wrote plays having a strong motive of entertainment, designed to please themselves, to show off their linguistic and dialectical skills, and to express life as they thought it was or should be lived. Their heroes did not have to be morally good but only artistically good—good fighters, good thinkers, good leaders or possessed of some outstanding quality which took them out of the ranks of common men and demonstrated what the Greeks called *arete* or the ability of a champion. This book concerns mediæval drama which is, in a number of ways, different from Renaissance drama, although it is obvious that *Henry V* did not just grow out of nothing and that Marlowe's *Tamburlaine* is not to be explained simply as a breath of fresh air, a new departure, or the arrival of an enlightened genius who swept away the cobwebs and gave us poetic drama for the first time. Recent studies of Elizabethan play-writing, and especially of Shakespeare's art, have shown how 'mediæval' a man Shakespeare really was and how much he depended on old-established ideas and conventions; we learn a good deal about dramatic traditions in *A Midsummer Night's Dream* and *Hamlet*, in which there are scattered references to acting; or in *Twelfth Night*, where the action is introduced and broken by music and song. But mediæval drama is not poetic drama, and the English of the Elizabethan play is much more subtle and developed than the limited vocabulary of earlier plays. Characters have begun to express themselves in images, metaphors and complicated figures, and much of the action lies in the talk. Tamburlaine is a talker, a talker in *hyperbole*. Listen to him near the beginning of the play:

> I hold the Fates bound fast in iron chains,
> And with my hand turn Fortune's wheel about:
> And sooner shall the sun fall from his sphere
> Than Tamburlaine be slain or overcome.
> Draw forth thy sword, thou mighty man-at-arms,
> Intending but to raze my charmed skin,
> And Jove himself will stretch his hand from Heaven
> To ward the blow and shield me safe from harm . . .

I, 2, 173–80

and near the end:

16

> The god of war resigns his room to me,
> Meaning to make me general of the world.
> Jove, viewing me in arms, looks pale and wan,
> Fearing my power should pull him from his throne.
> Where'er I come the Fatal Sisters sweat,
> And grisly Death, by running to and fro,
> To do their ceaseless homage to my sword . . .
>
> TAMBURLAINE THE GREAT, Part I. V, 2, 388–94

Tamburlaine's arrogant and grossly overpowering personality is here expressed not only by what he says but in the way he says it. He dwells consistently on certain images: conquest, destruction, carnage, torture, rapine, death, plunder, jewels, gold and silver, the human and material spoils of war; and the other characters, who are all minor, talk obsessively of Tamburlaine's invincibility so that he towers above them, a menacing figure of vast proportions who strikes terror not only into all men, but also into the gods of heaven and hell. Tamburlaine emerges as a stage superman and what he does is always subordinated to what he says. The minimum of concrete statement, a proliferation of dazzling, colourful images, like:

> Zenocrate, lovelier than the love of Jove,
> Brighter than is the silver Rhodope,
> Fairer than whitest snow on Scythian hills . . .
>
> I, 2, 87–9

the sonorous use of place-names—a device of classical rhetoricians later employed to great effect by Milton—and the cosmic references to Tamburlaine's power:

> Our souls, whose faculties can comprehend
> The wondrous architecture of the world,
> And measure every wand'ring planet's course,
> Still climbing after knowledge infinite,
> And always moving as the restless spheres,
> Wills us to wear ourselves, and never rest,
> Until we reach the ripest fruit of all,
> That perfect bliss and sole felicity,
> The sweet fruition of an earthly crown.
>
> II, 7, 21–9

together make a picture of artistic beauty, a series of pageants rather than a continuous movement, a revelation of personal feeling conveyed in lyrical speeches gradually building up this single personage from a superman to an 'over-reacher' who puts himself above God.

Compare this with a speech taken from *Everyman*, a play composed late in the 15th century, about a hundred years before *Tamburlaine*, and note some of the differences.

Everyman: Alas I may well wepe with syghes depe
      Now have I no maner of company,
   To helpe me in my journey and me to kepe,
      And also my wrytynge is butt unredy.
  How shall I do now for to exscuse me?
    I wolde to God I had never be gete!
  To my soule a full grete profyte it had be,
     For now I fere paynes huge and grete!
  The tyme passeth, Lorde helpe that all wrought!
  For though I mourne it avayleth nought.
  The day passeth and is almoost ago,
  I wote not well what for to do.

It is obvious that this is limited in vocabulary, and has no classical references or fine-sounding geographical names to convey an idea of spaciousness; moreover the speaker, unlike Tamburlaine, is self-abasing and timid and lacks an individual plan of action. Take another example, this time from the 14th-century York play of the Creation, spoken by a character representing God.

  1. I am gracyus and grete, god withoutyn begynnyng,
     I am maker unmade, all mighte es in me,
   I am lyfe and way unto welth-wynnyng,
     I am formaste and fyrste, als I byd sall it be.
   My blyssyng o ble sall be blendyng,
     And heldand fro harme to be hydande,
    My body in blys ay abydande
  Unendande withoutyn any endyng.

  2. Sen I am maker unmade, and moste es of mighte,
     And ay sall be endeles, and noghte es but I,

Unto my dygnyte dere sall diewly be dyghte
   A place full of plente to my plesing at ply,
And therewith als wyll I have wroght
   Many dyvers doynges be-dene,
   Whilke warke sall mekely contene
And all sall be made even of noght.

This paraphrases the Scriptures, and is meant to be uttered in ringing tones; it is written in an alliterative verse-form, and derives its strength from a series of words beginning with the same letter or containing the same vowel-sounds, and shows a certain crude strength of purpose and inflexibility of will such as one might associate with the apocryphal Old Testament God if one were an illiterate, unsophisticated and untravelled peasant living in feudal Yorkshire six hundred years ago.

In the 1963 York Festival production, the actor who played God appeared with his features concealed by a hood which helped to banish his flesh-and-blood personality. There was some scenery, though very little that could be called elaborate, and the God-figure addressed his audience from a scaffold which later served as a high point from which Lucifer was cast down, first swelling with pride, then suddenly crying and complaining:

Owe! certes! what I am worthely wroghte with wyrshyp, i-wys!
   For in a glorious gle my gletering it glemes,
I am so mightyly made my mirth may noghte mys,
   Ay sall I byde in this blys thorowe brightnes of bemes.
Me nedes noghte of noy for to neven,
   All welth in my welde have I weledande,
   Abowne yhit sall I be beeldand,
On heghte in the hyeste of hewven.

Ther sall I set my selfe, full semely to seyghte,
   To ressayve my reverence thorowe right o renowne,
I sall be lyke unto hym that es hyeste on heghte;
   Owe! what I am derworth and defte—Owe! dewes! all goes
                          downe!
My mighte and my mayne es all marrande,
   Helpe! felawes, in faythe I am fallande.

and when he lands with a thump on the ground, he is in the inferno.

> Owte! owte! harrowe! helpless, slyke hote at es here,
> > This es a dongon of dole that I am to dyghte . . .

he wails, and a companion devil echoes his complaint:

> Owte! owte! I go wode for wo, my wytte is all wente nowe
> > All oure fode es but filth, we fynde us beforn,
> We that ware beelded in blys in bale are we brent nowe,
> > Owte! on þe Lucifer, lurdan! oure lyghte has thu lorne.
> Þi dedes to this dole nowe has dyghte us,
> > To spille us þu was oure spedar,
> > For thow was oure lyghte and oure ledar,
> The hegheste of heven hade þu hyght us.

This is almost, but not quite, the stuff of burlesque. It appeals
to the visual and aural faculties and hardly at all to the intellect,
for it was meant to bring to life an accepted theological truth and
show it in striking terms to an audience who were there to be
educated first and entertained second.

DRAMA AND THE CHURCH

The primary aim of mediæval drama was to show man the path
to Redemption, and it did so by teaching, through the eye and
the ear, the doctrine of Repentance, which was the key to salvation in a society believing in Original Sin. After the Fourth
Lateran Council of 1215 it was required of all Christians that
they went to confession and communion at least once yearly or
suffer minor excommunication. The Church, however, recog-
nised that neither the priests nor the canon law were strong
enough to make people perform this duty, and this is why a
movement was started to instruct both clergy and people in the
doctrine of Repentance. In the course of the 13th century a
campaign of reform developed among the priests, who had been
remarkably ignorant men knowing little of theology. During
the late Middle Ages emphasis was placed on preaching and penitence, and there was a constant repetition, by itinerant friars,
of sermons on the Commandments, the Seven Sacraments, the
Creed and the Seven Deadly Sins. Through such exhortations
it was hoped that the individual conscience might be stirred to

self-examination, and the titles of contemporary religious treatises and handbooks show the trend—the *Lay Folks' Mass Book* and *Catechism*, the *Manual of Sins*, Mirk's *Festial* and *Instructions for Parish Priests*, the *Cursor Mundi*, a digest of Bible stories, and most popular of all, the *Pricke of Conscience*. There were many such works, dealing with vices and virtues, remorse, hardness of heart, interference with grace and penance; they reflected the designs of religious orders like the Dominicans and Franciscans to educate and reform. Religious drama developed at the same time, and the miracle play cycles were arranged to show Man's fallen nature through the Old Testament episodes, and to light the way of his salvation according to contemporary theological doctrine by means of scenes chosen from the New Testament. Cain is the first impenitent, eternally damned; the sacrifice arranged for Isaac prefigures the Crucifixion; the Harrowing of Hell suggests the power to erase sin; the Resurrection of Lazarus is a dramatic sermon on repentance; and the scourging and buffeting scenes in the Passion plays were intended to fix mediæval man's mind on the need to repent before confronting him with the Final Judgment, the last play in each of the cycles.

The staging of these plays was thought of as mirroring human history, starting with the Creation, considered as a great drama—the 'human comedy' in fact. One way of looking at a typical miracle cycle assumes that it was an acted sermon on repentance, complete with examples, exhortations, meditations, and colourful illustrations, and in various ways carrying over the argumentative techniques of the mediæval preacher. The castigation of folly, the impassioned prophecy of doom, the flashes of laughter and pathos, and the highly individual manner of presentation all indicate the close association of sacred oratory with sacred drama. But the relation of both to a rigid body of doctrine tells us that the religious drama *answered* man's questions, whereas a Shakespearean play *asked* questions but gave no explicit answers.

But we are looking too far ahead. The miracle cycles were a mature growth, the result of two hundred years of change marked by several clearly perceptible stages. Mediæval drama was not a reappearance, after centuries, of a dormant classical tradition, but a new birth. Out of the liturgy came the *trope*, out of the *trope* came the ritual-drama or *ordo* with several scenes, and out of the *ordo* was developed the *ludus*. *Ludus* is the Latin word for play and, properly speaking, what we are seeking is not *drama* but *ludus*, a play having a Latin text. At some later period of development, the medium of communication changed from Latin to the local vernacular, e.g. French or English or German or Italian. Such a species of drama, with a text, and invented *personae*, performed on a stage by laymen outside the church-door, had a 'secular' as distinct from a 'religious' character, so that although the themes were mainly taken from the Scriptures, the conventions governing their representation were not those of the liturgy. *Liturgy*, like *drama*, is also of Greek origin, and refers to the text of a religious service. 'Liturgical drama' is thus rather a loose way of referring to the *ludi* or plays which were the result of a gradual process of secularisation. Any discussion of the evolution of the *ludus* must start with a reference to the liturgy of the Catholic Church, an ancient set of ritual formularies having a lengthy and complicated history and centred on the service which we call the Mass, the essence of which is a representation of The Last Supper.

2

Liturgical Drama

Nowadays we think of the Mass as worship, not drama, and historians of the theatre have generally been rather wary of discussing religion and literature in the same terms. In fact, religious ritual *was* the drama of the 8th, 9th and 10th centuries and the services of the Christian Church and the liturgical drama which developed out of them cannot be kept apart. Early in the 9th century, Amalarius, Bishop of Metz, a personage conspicuous at the court of Charlemagne, wrote several interpretations of the Mass. One of these, the *Liber officialis*, had a far-reaching influence, traceable in devotional manuals as late as the 12th century.

Amalarius took upon himself to explain the Mass (in its early mediæval form) to the people at large or *simpliciores*, 'the simpler folk', so that his readings may be considered as early essays in dramatic criticism not to be eschewed by modern students repelled by the theological or scholastic atmosphere in which they were originally composed. What Amalarius did was to present the Mass as an elaborate drama. The participants were role-players, acting out a plot of which the ultimate importance lay in its re-creation of the life, crucifixion and resurrection of Christ, through which the divine plan of redemption was restored.

His interpreters were thus made to understand the Mass as a vital dramatic form and they carried on his work, issuing many complicated explanations of this ceremony, independent of one another and markedly inconsistent, but all having the recollective allegory in common. Modern critics concur in that the Mass displays important similarities to the dramatic rituals practised by primitive societies (to which reference is made in the next chapter). It clearly draws from the universal fund of archetypes or inherited mental images and the experience which it conveys may only be explained in dramatic terms. Mr. O. B. Hardison's recent *Christian Rite and Christian Drama in the Middle Ages* examines the Mass as sacred drama and by doing so welds a strong link joining the cultural activities of the 9th century to those of the 12th, for the ritual structure of the Mass and the Church year was carried over into later European representational plays, such as the *Mystère d'Adam*, *Ludus Danielis* and eventually the Corpus Christi cycle. These plays had a consistent formal pattern imposed upon them which, as Hardison observes, goes a long way towards bridging the awkward gap separating mediæval from Renaissance drama, a gap hitherto inadequately accounted for on historical principles of gradual evolution.

Apart from the Mass itself, the earliest manifestation of a distinct dramatic entity was the *trope*, a generic name for a literary or musical addition to the authorised liturgical text. The word comes from another Greek word meaning 'turn' and troping first began as a mnemonic device to enable choirs to remember the words of the service. Since the liturgy was being interpreted as a symbolic representation of Christ's life, extra-liturgical embellishment, mime, movement, ritual action, processional, singing, the playing of musical instruments and the growth of gorgeous ceremonial against a cathedral background of artistic activity were all given a powerful incentive. In his *Inferno*, Dante called art 'the grandchild of God', recalling Pope Gregory the Great's statement, made in one of his *Dialogues*, to the effect that the Mass was a visible (or 'literal') reflection of the invisible; its surrounding beauties were intended to make the worshippers feel ennobled. Notre Dame de Chartres, Rheims, Beauvais, Laon, Canterbury, York and Lincoln, to name seven of the more magnificent architectural monuments of the Gothic period, each combined spires, pillars, vaulting and the finest wood- and metal-work that craftsmen could produce to give emphasis to the binding relationship between the creations of Man and of God. The wonderful stained-glass windows of

Notre Dame de Chartres, consecrated in 1260, re-enacted the whole story of Man from the Creation to the Final Judgment, an immense pageant dedicated to the Virgin which endures even to this day. Over a century earlier, in 1130, there took place the dedication ceremony of the new choir of Canterbury Cathedral, attended by Henry I and his retinue. The congregation chanted: 'Awesome is this place. Truly this is the house of God and the gate of Heaven, and it will be called the court of the Lord', and Henry, transported at the sight of the choir, 'swore with his royal oath "by the death of God" that truly it was awesome'. For him it was Heaven's threshold. Nowhere may the dramatic qualities of the liturgy be seen to better advantage than in a Gothic cathedral, 'the symbol of the Kingdom of God on earth'.

MUSIC AND LITURGY

When we talk of the 12th century in connection with mediæval artistic endeavour, we are touching the high point of an intellectual movement fostered by Charlemagne during the 8th century, and approved by Pope Gregory the Great in the 6th century. Gregory perceived the value of painting as a medium of instruction for people who could not read and, following the authority of St. Augustine, encouraged the use of music in churches. St. Augustine, meditating on the mystery of Redemption, was convinced that *harmony* properly expressed to human ears Christ's work of reconciliation; for him it was an echo of theological truth, and he believed that the enjoyment which our senses derive from musical harmony was our intuitive response to ultimate reality. This explains why, although Augustine's views on art were extremely puritanical, music became a subject for study and cultivation even in the more ascetic monastic orders, such as the Cistercian. His musical mysticism, allied to a similar feeling about arithmetic, with its 'ratios' and 'congruences', provided a rich metaphorical store for later mediæval writers who tried to describe heavenly bliss in terms of angel choirs. More fundamentally, it influenced theologians during the 12th and 13th centuries to regard musical experience and artistic composition, especially in cathedral architecture, as being closely linked. Augustine's authority thus stretched from beginning to end of the Middle Ages. Adapted from various sources, including Greek, Roman, Hebrew, Oriental, Moslem and Provençal, music developed within the liturgy until by the 13th century the high peak of mediæval hymnody, exemplified by *Dies Irae* and *Stabat Mater*, had been attained. The rhythmical hymn *Te Deum* goes back 900 years before that, and must have been heard by Augustine himself.

Before 1200 music was of the simplest monophonic kind, capable of being sung by average performers in unison with a smoothly-continuous rhythm. This *musica plana* or 'plainsong' was made uniform by the authority of the *Schola Cantorum* in Rome, who sent out trained teachers to the different choir schools. Nowadays we call this plainsong 'Gregorian chant', and in the Roman Catholic Church it is still the official liturgical music. While the liturgical drama was evolving, therefore, hymns and chants formed an integral part of the Christian service, and it was during this period, called by historians the 'Carolingian Renaissance', that 'troping' started, at first as a short extension but soon lengthened as the result of experiment. Of the earliest tropes, that on *Alleluia* provides a convenient example. It was sung, together with a verse, during the introductory portion of the Mass, and the custom developed of singing the final *a* vowel to an elaborate serpentine melody, interpreted by ecclesiastical symbolists as an expression of human yearning for the after-life. Similar treatment was probably given to *Gloria in excelsis Deo* and to *Kyrie eleison* (Lord, have mercy), a Greek survival in the Latin liturgy. The melody grew so long that it was eventually divided into shorter sections known as *sequences* which were given words; there were hundreds of sequences, written first in prose, then in verse, in a variety of metrical patterns. They were mostly utterances of jubilation, and some of the more ambitious ones have considerable literary merit. Many show dramatic promise, since they include fragments of dialogue, but these were, with one exception, not acted out. This exception is the *Quem Quaeritis* of

Easter Day, and it is from this Easter Trope, rather than from the Mass itself, that historians of the English mediæval drama usually take their starting-point.

This Easter Trope is contained in a 10th-century manuscript from the Swiss monastery of St. Gall. It is based upon the Gospel account of the question 'Whom seek ye in the sepulchre?' addressed by the angel to the Marys at Christ's tomb, followed by the angel's announcement to them of the fact of Resurrection. It is in dialogue form, unlike any of the Gospel accounts, so that one can only speculate at the precise origins of the author's inspiration—possibly the Passion according to St. John. In the course of this the following is chanted by the deacon:

> Quem quaeritis?
> Responderunt ei:
> Jesum Nazarenum.
>
> Quem quaeritis?
> Illi autem dixerunt:
> Jesum Nazarenum.

It is reasonable, therefore, to regard the Easter Trope as an original composition. It was originally sung as a choral addition to the music of the Introit of the Mass, coming at the end of Lauds, the first of the *horae* or day-hours of the Church, and there were several variants. The English version in the *Regularis Concordia* or Harmony of the Rule, compiled under the direction of Æthelwold, Bishop of Winchester, about 970, was a very full one, heavily supported by stage directions, suggesting that the author wished to make quite certain that the lines would be dramatised as well as sung uniformly in all Benedictine monasteries. In the *Regularis Concordia* it is made clear that the purpose of such ceremonies was to fortify the faith of the vulgar and unlearned. There are more than 400 surviving versions of this *Visitatio Sepulchri*, distributed in most European countries, including France, Italy, Spain, England, Germany and Poland, both in manuscript and later in printed form. Before the end of the 10th century the Winchester Cathedral trope had grown into a self-contained liturgical drama, forming part of the 3rd Nocturn of Matins on Easter morning. Here is a quotation from the last part:

> While the third lesson is being chanted, let four brothers vest themselves, one of whom, vested in an alb (a long white garment), enters as if to do something, and, in an inconspicuous way, approaches the place where the sepulchre is, and there, holding a palm in his hands, sits quiet. While the third respond is chanted, let the three others approach, all alike vested in copes, bearing thuribles (incense-holders) with incense in their hands, and, with hesitating steps, in the semblance of persons seeking something, let them come before the place of the sepulchre. These things are done, indeed, in representation of the angel sitting within the tomb and of the women who come with spices to anoint the body of Jesus. When, therefore, he who is seated sees the three approaching as if wandering about and seeking something, let him begin to sing melodiously and in a voice moderately loud,

> Quem quaeritis in sepulchro, O Christicolae?
> (Whom do you seek in the tomb, O lovers of Christ?)

> When this has been sung to the end, let the three respond in unison,

> Iesum Nazarenum crucifixum, O caelicola.
> (Jesus of Nazareth, him that was crucified, O heavenly one.)

> Then he,

> Non est hic. Surrexit, sicut praedixerat. Ite, nuntiate quia surrexit a mortuis.
> (He is not here. He has risen as he had prophesied. Go, announce that he has risen from the dead.)

> Upon the utterance of this command, let the three turn to the choir and say, Alleluia, resurrexit Dominus!
> (Alleluia, the Lord has risen!)

> This said, let him, still remaining seated, say, as if calling them back, the anthem
> Venite, et videte locum ubi positus erat Dominus. Alleluia.
> (Come and see the place where the Lord was laid. Alleluia.)

This is clearly a 'play' distinct from the original trope, which became detached from its position in the procession of the Mass and was inserted in the services preceding the Mass. In course of time, the *Quem Quaeritis* dialogue was itself enlarged by adding further dialogue and action, and short plays of the same kind appropriate to occasions in other seasons were attached, so as to make a longer play with a series of scenes. The 400 versions of the *Visitatio* indicate the progression of stages through which this trope became a fully-developed play by adding the characters of the Apostles Peter and John and, later, the resurrected Christ, and providing relevant dialogue and action. The most elaborate literary version is the 12th-century one from the play-book of the monastery of St. Benoît-sur-Loire at Fleury, based on the St. John Gospel, and written in a mixture of prose and verse. It is occasionally revived, as, for example, in Coventry Cathedral in April 1963, where it was strikingly presented in a social and aesthetic context profoundly different from that in which it was conceived. In another complicated version, handed down in an early 13th-century German manuscript, Pilate sets a watch before the tomb, at the request of the Jewish high priests, to stop the disciples from taking away Christ's body. The angel with his flaming sword appears and strikes down the soldiers, and only at this point is the visitation scene played. The soldiers are given another scene after the Marys depart in which they tell of their experiences and reveal that Christ's body has been stolen by the disciples. The introduction of the soldiers, from the St. Matthew Gospel, was another late refinement, and marked the final expansion of the original trope.

The Christmas play of the Nativity was acted around the *praesepe* or manger, first depicted in a crude fashion and later in the form of a tableau, with Joseph, Mary, the ox and the ass, as in Catholic churches today. A variant trope, *Quem Quaeritis in Praesepe*, originally used in the Introit of the Third or Great Mass and later transferred to Matins, seems to have been the source of this play. At some stage it became part of an Epiphany play about the visit of the Magi, with the focal point a star hung from the nave and lighted by candles—sometimes the star was a movable one, drawn by cords so that the Magi could follow it about. This was another distinct play, with priest-actors impersonating the Magi. In some of these Nativity scenes, Herod first makes his appearance. Herod was later to cut an important figure in the miracle cycles, but the ranting irascible monarch of the St. Matthew Gospel and ecclesiastical tradition first strutted before an audience in this French Nativity play of the 11th century. In later plays Herod shows himself in his traditional role as the enraged butcher of the male children around Bethlehem.

With the increased dramatic action, stage properties grew more complicated. The sepulchre might have been fashioned at first from prayer-books, or a recessed tomb could have been used, but later a more realistic and even a permanent sepulchre, such as may still be seen in mediæval churches, was constructed to aid the regular performance of these plays. Music, processional and scenic effects added depth to what had become a performance in its own right, separated from the liturgy, and the Gospel scenes were enhanced by secular additions, taken from *lectiones*, or liturgical readings, containing biblical passages and homilies. One such *lectio*, believed erroneously during the Middle Ages to be the work of St. Augustine, was called *Contra Judæos, Paganos, et Arianos Sermo de Symbolo*; in it the homilist first calls upon the Jews to behold the coming of Christ, citing the prophets in order and then calling again upon the Gentiles to bear similar witness. The content and wide popularity of this sermon is less important for our purposes than the fact that it, and not a trope, provided the source of the *Prophet Play*.

This play, designated *Ordo Prophetarum*, or *Prophetae*, is a dialogue, introducing a succession of prophets, Israel, Moses, Isaiah, Jeremiah, Daniel, Habakkuk, David, Simeon, Elisabeth, John the Baptist, Virgil, Nebuchadnezzar and the Erythræan Sibyl, each dressed appropriately and carrying identifying symbols, taken from the conventions of religious art, so that Moses had his tablets of law, David his sling, Daniel his lion and so on. One 13th-century version of the *Ordo* supplies precise stage directions indicating the physical appearance of each prophet, and it is evident that the play represents a transitional

30

development between the church ritual of the liturgy and the *ludus*. Some versions are more obviously ritualistic than others, and their exact relationship to the original *lectio* varied from one version to the next. The dramatic scheme—a procession of saints in conventional garb and uttering conventional speeches—lent itself to monotony, and it may readily be understood why the clergy added dramatic action to what Karl Young, in *The Drama of the Mediæval Church*, calls 'an unrelieved succession of summonings and respondings'. It is possible that certain of the episodes, having developed in a literary-dramatic direction, detached themselves from the *Ordo Prophetarum* and survived as independent religious plays. This theory, first propounded nearly a century ago by Marius Sepet, a French historian of the theatre, suggests that the independent plays were later reassembled as cycles; and this is one explanation of the origins of the vernacular cycles as a whole, as well as of extant single plays about prophets like Daniel, Abraham or Moses. It is now held that the liturgy itself produced the cyclical form, which enables a complete re-enactment of Christ's life to be presented as one play.

'THE PLAY OF DANIEL'

One such play, *Ludus Danielis*, which may well have antecedents of the kind suggested above, has come down to us as one of the best examples of liturgical drama proper. It is especially interesting because it is the only *ludus* so far transcribed into modern musical notation. This modern transcription, by an American Benedictine, Fr. Rembert Weakland, was first performed in January 1958, in the cloisters of the Metropolitan Museum of New York, and was the first recorded performance since the late Middle Ages. In summer 1960, *Daniel* was played at Wells, Oxford, and most impressively in Westminster Abbey. W. H. Auden provided a modern verse adaptation of the original Latin text, and the musicians, the New York *Pro Musica*, played on modern reproductions of mediæval instruments. Music and the early drama were thus shown to have been drawn together in a coherent relationship by the year of *Daniel*'s composition, that is to say, about 1180.

From poetry and contemporary pictures we have collected some information about the impressive range of instruments used by mediæval musicians. Guillaume de Machaut in a poem called *Remede de Fortune* gives a list of them. Some are of Arabic origin:

Viële, rubebe, guiterne,
Leu, morache, michanon,
Citole et la psalterion,
Harpe, tabour, trompes, naquaires,
Orgues, cornes, plus de di paires,
Cornemuses, flajos, chevrettes,
Tymbre, la flaüste d'Alemaingne,
Flajos de saus, fistule, pipe,
Muse d'Aussay, trompe petite
Buisines, eles, monocorde
Ou il n'a c'une seule corde,
Et muse de blef tout ensemble.

In the percussion group, there were, for example, bells, cymbals, jingles, timbrels, triangle, bombulum, and large and small drums. In the strings, the lyre, cithera, harp, psaltery, noble, organistrum, lute, guitar, vielle (a short violin played with a curved bow), viola, monochord, gigue, and rebec. Wind instruments included the pipe, flute, hautboy, bagpipe, clarion, flageolet, trumpet, horn and the portative organ. As far back as the 9th century the Venerable Bede referred to organs 'with brass pipes filled with air from bellows, and uttering a grand and most sweet melody'. Illuminations on mediæval manuscripts of the 13th century depict instrumentalists; sometimes devils are also included, leering over the shoulders of the players and reminding us that musicians had to be absolved before taking part in plays. St. Augustine's musical mysticism did not prevent the art of playing an instrument from being considered less than respectable as a profession, so that musicians preferred to keep on the right side of ecclesiastical law. In a 14th-century window in the nave of York Minster two monkeys, the symbols of unseemly levity and indecorous behaviour, may be seen playing musical instruments as part of the Great Choir of Creation.

In spite of intensive research by musicologists, who have at their disposal many original manuscripts, a good deal of mystery still surrounds mediæval music and it is a matter of guesswork how the composers intended it to sound. Experts who have tried to transcribe it into modern musical notation disagree among themselves, particularly about rhythmic intention, for mediæval music is very complicated, with long syncopated passages and remarkably little indication to help a modern performer to play them accurately. But we now understand and appreciate that early liturgical drama is a musical phenomenon and its music is, at long last, receiving careful attention. Present-day students of drama history no longer have to imagine what these early plays were like, for a number of them may be witnessed in performance or heard in recorded versions which, even if they may represent a synthetic divorce from their real context of Christian worship, also do a great deal to bring the otherwise remote to life.

The *Daniel* manuscript, a 13th-century copy kept in the British Museum, tells us at the beginning that it was composed by students of the Choir School at Beauvais:

Ad honorem tui Christe
Danielis ludus iste
In Belvaco est inventus
Et invenit hunc iuventus.

It was a composite production, a communal effort having no single composer. One Beauvais student started by making a trope, which his fellows expanded. Beauvais was known in the 12th century as an experimental centre. Radulphus or Raoul, pupil of the famous Abelard, taught there, and the school was sometimes reprimanded because of its enthusiasm for 'pagan', that is, Latin, poetry. There is certainly a 'popular' quality about *Daniel* which suggests the influence of Radulphus, but the play is not completely original and was most probably an enlarged version of a prophet play by another of Abelard's pupils, the wandering English scholar Hilarius, known also as the author of plays on *The Raising of Lazarus* and on St. Nicholas. There are many similarities connecting the two plays, but the Beauvais *Daniel* is dramatically superior. Karl Young provides a detailed comparison in the second volume of his *Drama of the Mediæval Church*.

Although there was a developing polyphony at Beauvais, *Daniel* has a monophonic, non-contrapuntal setting, suggesting, perhaps, that liturgical drama was customarily performed without any attempt at harmonisation, thus allowing individual singers more freedom to develop their *motifs*. The part of Daniel has obvious attractions for a good tenor soloist and offers considerable scope for interpretation, especially in the lamentation scene, when Daniel gives himself up for lost:

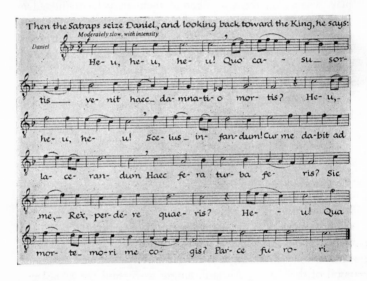

And as he is thrust into the pit with the lions:

> For this charge I am not guilty:
> Have mercy on me, O God;
>   eleison.
> Send, O God, a protector here
> To restrain the lions' power;
>   eleison.

In fact, the play as a whole is akin to opera. Though it was not primarily intended to do anything but 'touch the mysteries' it becomes essentially a work of art in terms of modern aesthetic theory because it presents an audience with a unique kind of spectacle. The scoring connects certain instruments with certain personages—the psaltery, harp and organ accompany and suggest the holy figures, the trumpet ushers in the king and those who address him, the recorder, bells, vielle and percussion are all linked to the pagan courts, and the rebec, which has a nasal sound, is associated with the envious counsellors who poison the mind of Darius against Daniel. The play ends with a verse of the hymn *Nuntium vobis fero de supernis* foretelling the birth of Christ, and the *Te Deum*, which confirms the liturgical origins of the whole. There is a strong Oriental character in the music, which reflects the Eastern elements in the Gregorian chant and perhaps the indirect influence of the Crusades.

The impression made by this play is hard to convey, though a recording goes a long way to bring home the immense power of a dramatic form practically unknown to the modern world. The playing-time is less than an hour, there are a dozen processions, and scope for magnificent costuming, lyrical singing, attention to staging details and character-interpretation. The display of choral and instrumental skill is there to be enjoyed. As performed in Westminster Abbey, this colourful re-enactment of *Daniel* immediately linked the London audience with the Beauvais School of eight centuries ago and its youthful enthusiasm for making a popular attraction out of this well-known Bible story. It should be remembered that the Daniel episode so far as Radulphus and his disciples were concerned was a part of history. What they were doing was to enhance facts with the aid of music and lively acting and, by making a play with a strong ritual character, to convey the inevitability of events in as striking a manner as was possible at that time.

Daniel demonstrates that so far as dramatic art was concerned, a high degree of enlightenment existed in France by the 12th century, suggesting in its turn that something of the same reaching for perfection filtered through to England. The influence of a play in which musical skill and dramatic action were so success-fully united cannot be easily estimated now, since musicianship was rare outside abbey choir schools and instruments were hard to obtain outside the cloister where many of them were con-structed. Liturgical drama cannot really be described as strongly 'popular', though in the case of *Daniel* it does contain popular elements, such as the angel's seizing of Habakkuk by the hair, which has about it a goliardic sense of the absurd, and the adaptation to liturgical purposes of the rhythms and tunes of the *trouvères* or wandering minstrels of France. In the rhyming Latin, occasional French phrases occur, as when Daniel, summoned to Darius, utters the words '*Pauper et exulans en vois al Roi par vos*'.

Any notion that mediæval liturgical drama was dull was banished during the first few minutes of this colourful recon-struction of a fully-developed example of the form. As *The Times* reviewer remarked of the Westminster Abbey perform-ance, *Daniel* had 'a strong visual and aural appeal which will commend it to those who have no special liking for things mediæval . . .' which was presumably meant to be generous praise. It is this superficially opera-like character which distinguishes the full liturgical drama from the vernacular mystery plays which started to make their appearance in the early part of the 12th century. These have been called 'semi-liturgical' which is as convenient a term as any, since although these plays continued as an appendage to the church service, their connection was loose and their sources were a complex mixture of sacred history, saints' lives, sermons, apocryphal writings and ill-defined traditions.

SECULAR TRENDS

There were many such plays, in numerous versions, and although extant material is scanty, it is clear that there existed in Europe from about 1100 a thriving drama having liturgical origins, especially active in France, Germany and Italy, which marked the inception of a new era of play-making. Any strictly religious aim was short-lived, and secularism is evident almost from the beginning of the movement. Well-rooted objections on the part of the Church to the association of its members with acting and music seem in the long run to have been ineffective. Instructive entertainment based upon well-known Bible stories, performed by capable members of the clergy, assisted by laymen and singers who had, presumably, abandoned their former wickednesses and repented of their sins, provided a powerful counter-attraction. The Church may be said to have consecrated the play to its own use, though there were, as might be expected, many differing opinions on what should and should not be done when portions of the liturgy were dramatised. There were numerous instances of ecclesiastical personages overdoing their enthusiasm, and of other, usually elderly, ecclesiastical personages reproving them, as happened when a Florentine monk wrote a piece about Adam and Eve and played the part of Adam himself, stark naked. St. Thomas Aquinas was more lenient than most. He said that the profession of *histrio* or actor was ordained for the solace of humanity and that with God's mercy an actor might still escape the punishment of Hell. Bishop Grosstête of Lincoln, writing in the middle of the 13th century, was a much harsher critic and condemned all drama outright, even those plays containing no specifically secular material. Robert Mannyng of Brunne complained about 'miracles' in *Handlyng Synne* (1303), but he seems to have been thinking of two kinds of play: one, the Easter and Nativity plays, performed by priests within the church and permissible; and the others, also performed by priests, but taking place outside the church 'in ways or graves', that is, in the streets or in the churchyard: these were worthy only of censure.

'THE MYSTERY PLAY OF ADAM'

A strongly secular development is apparent, and fortunately there is an excellent example of a play which fills this historical gap. Unlike *Daniel*, it is a vernacular Anglo-Norman play, composed less than half a century earlier than the Beauvais masterpiece. This play is called *Le Mystère d'Adam* and it is the first example of the secular popular drama, performed by a trained cast. The incomplete Tours manuscript has elaborate stage directions in Latin, instructing the actors how to play their parts, and the emotional effect of the play is theatrical rather than liturgical. Mr. Arnold Williams in *Drama of Mediæval England* compares its temptation scene with Milton's treatment in Book IX of *Paradise Lost* and offers an account of this delicate character-study rendered into colloquial modern English. Diabolus appeals to Eve's pride, vanity and ambition, saying that he wants to help her better herself and flattering her with calculated cunning. He offers to reveal a wonderful secret to her if she will promise to keep it, and gives the impression that by trusting her with this secret he will be putting himself in her power. He undermines Adam's character, suggesting that he is stupid and obstinate, whereas she, Eve, is wise and full of tenderness, fresher than a rose, whiter than a snowflake. Diabolus then transfers his attack to the Creator who caused such an ill-assorted couple to be joined together. This leads the tempter with apparent logic to the garden and its forbidden fruit which, he says, will release Eve from her bondage and make her Queen of the World, Heaven and Hell, and mistress of universal knowledge. With a final touch of cleverness he sums up such an achievement as being no more than her physical charms deserve.

Step by step Eve gives ground until at last she eats the fruit. Adam is harder to convince and at first rejects any encouragement to follow Eve's example in disobeying the Creator. As the pair are arguing, a serpent rears up behind the Tree of Knowledge and Eve pretends to listen to its counsel. Then she offers the apple to Adam, taunting him and doubting his courage while she extols the qualities of the fruit, its flavour and incomparable sweetness. So Adam falls a victim to Eve's seduction, and, lamenting, they are expelled from Eden. The dialogue is extremely subtle and invites the talents of good actors, particularly since the part of Eve would have been taken by a male to whom the description '*fieblette*' or 'delicate little thing' might not have easily applied.

The second act, or part, is about Cain's murder of Abel: it is an interesting example of early realism in stage dialogue:

Cain:	Abel, you are dead.
Abel:	And why?
Cain:	I want to have my revenge on you.
Abel:	Have I done something wrong?
Cain:	Yes, a great wrong. You are a traitor and the fact is well proven.
Abel:	Certainly not.
Cain:	Do you deny it?
Abel:	I shall never commit an act of treason.
Cain:	You did!
Abel:	How did I?
Cain:	You'll know soon enough.
Abel:	I do not understand.
Cain:	I shall soon let you know.
Abel:	You will never be able to prove that it's true.
Cain:	The proof is at hand.
Abel:	God will help me.
Cain:	I shall kill you.
Abel:	God will know it.

Then Cain shall raise his right hand and threaten him saying:

Cain:	Here is the proof of it.
Abel:	All my faith is in God.
Cain:	He won't be of much use against me.
Abel:	He can easily put a hindrance in your way.
Cain:	He cannot rescue you from death.
Abel:	I put myself wholly in his hands.
Cain:	Do you want to hear why I'm going to kill you?
Abel:	Tell me then.
Cain:	I shall tell you. You became too intimate with God; because of you he has refused me everything; because of you he refused my offering. Do you think I shan't pay you what you deserve? I'm going to give you your reward. Today you'll lie dead on the ground.

Cain then proceeds to beat Abel to death. The stage directions say that Abel 'shall have a saucepan hidden beneath his clothes', presumably over his head, so that Cain can strike him with the traditional ass's jawbone without doing any damage. The effect of the dialogue, all in short lines, is to endow the piece with vivacity and to mark off the cynical Cain from the pious

Abel more and more clearly as the suspense heightens towards the climax of murder.

The third act is much closer to the liturgy than the first two, for it is a prophet play in the conventional pattern of which we have already spoken; but the author draws on other material as well so that his descriptions of the various prophets are not just casual stereotypes. Abraham, Moses, Aaron, David, Solomon, Balaam, Daniel, Habakkuk, Jeremiah, Isaiah, and Nebuchadnezzar are each introduced in turn, talking in what the playwright imagined to be his own individual character. The *ordo* section is linked to the play as a whole by Adam, who is referred to by five of the prophets as being destined for deliverance as the symbol of man's sufferings. The *ordo*, which is unfinished, reveals the same original spirit which animates the Adam and Cain sections of *Le Mystère*.

Le Mystère d'Adam may be performed today with close reference to the unknown author's intentions because of the painstaking instructions which accompany the text—these describe movements, costumes, facial expressions, mode of delivery, properties, colours of the principal actors' costumes, demeanour of Adam and Eve before and after the temptation and many other details which show that the playwright himself directed the whole performance. The editor of the first English edition of the play, first printed in 1918, M. Paul Studer, began his preface by remarking that 'for the last half-century no account of the drama in the Middle Ages, whether written from an English or a French standpoint, has seemed complete without at least a reference to the *Mystère d'Adam*'. Miss Grace Frank, in *The Mediæval French Drama*, ends her discussion of the play by saying 'no more entertaining and delightful example has survived of how the early mediæval theatre might achieve its purpose of making vivid to the laity the doctrines of the Church'.

OTHER FRENCH PLAYS OF THE 13TH CENTURY

Another play which no historian of early drama should pass over is Jean Bodel's *Jeu de Saint Nicolas*, written about 1200, just before its author contracted leprosy, which kept him from the Fourth Crusade. The conflict of the play together with its Eastern setting reflects Bodel's crusading enthusiasm, but it is a mainly secular drama about the intervention of a saint in human affairs; not a 'saint's play', like the St. Nicholas play of Hilarius referred to previously, but a strongly-plotted *trouvère* comedy, the oldest extant *jeu*; it owes something to Easter and Christmas plays on the same subject and contains many echoes from liturgical texts. Nevertheless, it is an original treatment. Its author was a civic official of Arras, a town known at the time as a broad-minded centre of culture, festivals and literary societies, an '*escole de tous biens entendre*', as an anonymous writer calls it.

The legend which Bodel makes the basis of his plot is the same one which Hilarius treated. An infidel tax-gatherer learns of the miracles performed by St. Nicholas and gives the saint his treasure for safe-keeping. When thieves steal the treasure, the infidel threatens the saint but St. Nicholas appears in person and forces the thieves to return their ill-gotten gains, whereupon the infidel embraces Christianity. Bodel turns the infidel into a pagan king, a character who rants and raves like Herod, and endows him with a group of supporters: a servile major-domo, a brutal gaoler and a quartet of Eastern potentates reminiscent of the Magi. These pagans and their followers fight a smaller number of Christians, whom they slaughter to the last man but one. This solitary survivor, Preudom, is the means by which St. Nicholas converts the pagans and causes their false god, Tervagan, to be thrown from the temple. The thieves are low-life tavern characters, presumably drawn from the author's experience, and their quarrelsome, drunken conversation is vividly topical. Each villain is distinct, with strengths and weaknesses of personality, and the rapid changes of scene from palace to tavern, to battle-scene, to prison and back to tavern again, together with the comic rogueries of the picturesque and engaging thieves make *Le Jeu de Saint Nicolas* a tragi-comedy far in advance of its time. Of it Miss Grace Frank says that 'the serious parts give the impression of sincerity and high purpose, the humorous scenes add happy realism and gay entertainment to an essentially religious theme'.

The only other surviving French miracle play is Rutebeuf's *Miracle de Théophile*, written about 1261 and based on a Greek legend incorporated in the liturgy in the 11th century. It concerns a 6th-century ecclesiastic called Theophilus who turned down the offer of a bishopric. The man who accepted it dispossessed Theophilus even of the humbler post which he occupied, and in disgrace he formed a compact with the Devil. Restored to his office, he repented after seven years and was saved by the intercession of the Virgin. Rutebeuf's play, an early example of the Faust story, depends for its effect on its pathetic lyrical qualities, which bring out the sufferings of Theophilus in an intensely personal way. There is not much invention of plot or character, but the author is an ingenious manipulator of figurative language and metrical patterns. The Faustian theme of *Le Miracle de Théophile*, the contention of Good and Evil for the possession of a soul, looks back to the early Christian Latin verses of Prudentius, of whom we shall hear more later, and forward to the English morality plays of the 15th century, and eventually to Marlowe's *Dr. Faustus*.

One other playwright contributed to the transition from religious to secular drama. His name was Adam le Bossu or Adam de la Halle, also from Arras, who wrote a play called *Le Jeu de la Feuillée* (*The Play of the Leafy Bower*) about 1276. It has an alternative title, *The Play of Adam*, suggesting its strongly-autobiographical character. Adam (the author, not the Adam of *Genesis*) planned to become a priest but is diverted from his ecclesiastical call by Sweet Marie, whom he marries. There are three loosely-connected scenes, very personal and topical, abounding in slapstick. The male characters are actual friends of the author, and the feminine roles include that of a loose woman, Dame Douche, and three fairies, all probably played by men, who sing and dance. There is a madman, a begging monk, a doctor, a merchant, a taverner and a clown in this Aristophanic comedy. Much of the satire is 'local' and is for that reason lost on us, but the general impact of the work is one of vigour. It does seem that *Le Jeu d'Adam* is a long way from *Le Mystère d'Adam*, since it contains no liturgical elements and in many respects looks forward to the low comedy produced in England during the early part of the 16th century (see Chapter 7). Adam le Bossu's piece was representative of the kind of play condemned even by more moderate clerics, but which, it must be admitted, was often written by a clergyman.

Le Bossu is better known as the writer of what musicologists have called 'the first French comic opera'. This is *Le Jeu de Robin et Marion*, a pastoral idyll in which a shepherdess, Marion, fights off the advances of a knight and encourages Robin, a shepherd. The knight takes his revenge by beating Robin, but Robin forgets his pains at the sight of Marion, and the play ends with dancing and singing. The play is an expanded form of a contemporary lyric style, the *pastourelle*, treating of rustic love, but its significance for us is that it is a secular musical drama, containing twenty-six songs, a unique survival from the 13th century. If *Le Jeu d'Adam* has something of *A Midsummer Night's Dream* about it, then *Robin and Marion* anticipates *As You Like It*.

We have little evidence of the character of English secular plays, though contemporary records show that they existed. The earliest English play seems to have been Geoffrey's *Ludus de Sancta Katerina*, made about 1100, for which Geoffrey, then at Dunstable, borrowed ecclesiastical costumes from the sacristan of St. Albans. Unfortunately these were destroyed by fire during the performance, and the story goes that Geoffrey, at that time a layman, was so upset that he became a monk at St. Albans. Later he became its Abbot. Saints' plays by Anglo-Norman authors, none of which are extant, were being written and performed in the 12th century on both sides of the Channel. Change from Latin to vernacular French is first seen in a French play called *Sponsus*, a liturgical piece about the Wise and Foolish Virgins, composed before 1100 and handed down in a bilingual manuscript. But of other changes, such as those from Gospel characters to invented characters, from ecclesiastical garb to actors' costumes, from priests playing roles to laymen impersonating free creations of Bible characters and non-theological personages brought in to add contemporaneity, we have only the knowledge summed up in accounts of a few plays like *Le*

Mystère d'Adam, *Le Jeu de Saint Nicolas*, *Le Miracle de Théophile* and the completely secular creations of Adam le Bossu which seem to have evolved independently, perhaps from the folk-myths preserved by the *jongleurs* or wandering minstrels. More generally there was the gradual movement of the religious drama from the interior to the exterior of the church, from the chancel reserved for the clergy and choir, through the aisles and out of the church door to the secular stage with its developed conventions and provision for an audience, a process probably spread over a lengthy period of time, accelerated in some parts of Europe, like Arras, retarded in others, like Lincoln, whose Bishop Grosstête made frequent complaints against trends in play-making and, furthermore, was in a position to enforce his objections.

This process of secularisation and gradual desertion of formality was a natural and understandable one, but the work of Adam le Bossu suggests that there must have been other influences modifying the development of drama at this stage. For want of a better description, literary historians have called these elusive agencies 'folk' or 'popular' elements. In the next chapter we shall try to isolate them and suggest how they may have combined with the more formal plays.

3

Popular and Literary Elements

Every human society has its folk-customs. Social anthropologists have laid the groundwork for a great deal of speculation on such survivals, including those affecting the development of what we call 'art forms'; and in recent years works like Sir James Frazer's *Golden Bough* and Miss Jessie L. Weston's *From Ritual to Romance* have come to be important influences on literary critics seeking to establish the nature of those motives, conscious and unconscious, which govern imaginative writing. Robert Graves's *The Greek Myths* defines true myth as 'the reduction to narrative shorthand of ritual mime performed on public festivals', and relates it to the drama which came to be the authority for tribal religious institutions in ancient Greece. Much of it is disguised history, interlaced with genuine mythic elements, and it is agreed that ancient European religious beliefs were remarkably uniform, based on worship of the maternal spirit, or mother-goddess, a universal symbol of growth, appearing in many different legends under many different names. We know her best as Aphrodite, Hera, Ceres or simply as Mother Earth, celebrated in holy songs which were in fact accompaniments to ritual mime.

In such combinations of dancing, singing and recitation we have the essential beginnings of a dramatic art which developed along strangely similar lines in widely-separated countries and even continents over many centuries. We have no evidence of contact between European and Central American cultures, but the mythic similarities are often so striking as to compel one to look favourably upon the romantic theory of the universality of primitive man. This theory suggests that a tendency to act comes naturally to him, and that high emotions, ideally the spontaneous expressions of uncorrupted people giving form to their thoughts, were the sources of dancing, music and poetry, especially of narrative poetry. A primitive worshipper crying to the sun or bowing down before his god in an act of obeisance would half-consciously execute certain gestures, such as arm movements or steps. These would be fixed in a certain order or pattern and performed at an agreed time, usually sunrise or noon. Sometimes a great event could be deliberately repeated and kept alive in the popular memory by the acting-out of its main incidents; this was a way of keeping records and expressing pride in the deeds of ancestors.

The dances, games and folk-plays extant in mediæval Europe often celebrated myths long-forgotten in their original forms but which came down to early Saxon times as unsubtle representations of the coming of spring, the death of winter, fertility, plenitude, ancient battles with the elements symbolising tribal survival, and the tension of individual combat. These ceremonies were strongly ritualistic, and the participants were required to execute certain prescribed movements. The sword-dance, a celebration of warfare, is one of these which still survives; another is the Maypole, first recorded in 1490, and now thought of as the centrepiece of a harmless children's game, but said by cultural anthropologists to have been a phallic symbol of generation. Hock-tie-ing or Hocking, a tripping up and binding of one sex by the other, was a well-established observance in the 15th century. A manuscript in the Bodleian Library refers to the Bishop of Worcester ordering the Cathedral Almoner, in April 1450, to suppress disgraceful sports and amusements on 'Hok' days. There were also the Plough Monday 'plays', including a sword-dance, which took place on the first Monday after Epiphany.

There were many rituals of this kind, some still kept alive in a few towns and villages in England, many more in European countries. They were inherited from an older paganism nurturing traditional peasant beliefs. Holy days, fairs, *festas* and village games once held to honour pagan deities became associated with

Christian saints' days. Palm Sunday Festivals, for instance, symbolise rebirth, and Easter Eggs are ancient fertility symbols. Pagan and Christian have become so intermingled in many of these ceremonies as to resist separation. In most European countries there are scores of examples of living rituals marking dates in the Christian year but having an indistinct pagan origin. The episode in Robert Mannyng's *Handlyng Synne* concerning 'The Dancers of Colbek' starts off with a reference to 'karolles, wrastlynges and somour games' and goes on to tell of the awful punishment visited on some young people who danced and sang in the churchyard in defiance of the priest's warning. It seems that such conduct, though considered sacrilegious, was not uncommon, for there are numerous references of the kind in mediæval writings. Tension between pagan dance and Christian Mass was still sufficiently marked in the 14th century to have inspired Mannyng to rewrite the Colbek story with a thinly-disguised contemporary reference and a stern injunction to obey the priest's orders.

THE FOLK-PLAY

Closely linked with the dramatic dance is the folk-play, performed by mummers or guisers. Surviving examples are impoverished versions of a dramatic entertainment that sprang straight from the native English soil before historical times. What remains of the St. George and Robin Hood plays is probably very different from what they must at one time have been. There are no recorded performances earlier than the 15th century and we do not even know what a 15th-century St. George play was really like, since the standard text is from an 1853 version, taken down verbatim at an actual performance in Oxfordshire. There are several accounts of such performances and at least twenty-seven versions, but the basic plot runs to pattern. The best-known reference to an actual performance is that given by Thomas Hardy in *The Return of the Native*, first published in 1878. Hardy's portrait is a first-hand one, and in making use of a pagan survival to help him create that timeless and all-pervading 'Wessex' atmosphere, the novelist sheds incidental light on the motives and acting-styles of those who took part in folk-plays. As he observes:

> A traditional pastime is to be distinguished from a mere revival in no more striking feature than in this, that while in the revival all is excitement and fervour, the survival is carried on with a stolidity and absence of stir which sets one wondering why a thing that is done so perfunctorily should be kept up at all. Like Balaam and other unwilling prophets, the agents seem moved by an inner compulsion to say and do their allotted parts whether they will or no. This unweeting manner of performance is the true ring by which, in this refurbishing age, a fossilized survival may be known from a spurious reproduction.
> II, 4

Hardy then gives an account of an actual performance, with half a dozen quotations from the speeches. Eustacia Vye enters:

> Here come I, a Turkish Knight,
> Who learnt in Turkish land to fight;
> I'll fight this man with courage bold:
> If his blood's hot I'll make it cold!
> II, 5

a challenge which is immediately taken up by Slasher, the Valiant Soldier, who retorts:

> If, then, thou art that Turkish Knight,
> Draw out thy sword, and let us fight!

Eventually St. George himself sweeps in, declaiming:

> Here come I, Saint George, the valiant man,
> With naked sword and spear in hand,
> Who fought the dragon and brought him to the slaughter,
> And by this won fair Sabra, the King of Egypt's daughter;
> What mortal man would dare to stand
> Before me with my sword in hand?

These traditional characters make up a strange collection and include, in various versions, King Alfred and his Queen, King William, Giant Blunderbore, Old King Cole with a wooden leg, and a Doctor. The play has clear dramatic form and falls into three parts, the 'presentation', in which the characters introduce themselves one by one, the drama itself, rooted in the story of St. George and the Dragon, and the *quête* or money collection. Sometimes there is a concluding sword-dance.

Throughout the centuries the St. George story has symbolised the victory of good over evil, and the play may also represent renewal of life in Spring and the defeat of Winter. The story appears in a 13th-century compilation called *Legenda Aurea*, and makes the saint's slaying of the dragon conditional upon the consent of 15,000 citizens to be baptised into the Christian faith. The folk-play indicates direct Christian influence when the adversary becomes a Turkish Knight with his face blackened, as in Hardy's version, and the hero a Crusader, at first killed, then brought to life by the Doctor, representing perhaps the resurrective powers of Christ.

Attempts by scholars to trace mediæval parallels between religious drama and this Mummers' Play have resulted in a great deal of speculation; many strong resemblances are evident in scenes and lines spoken by characters in morality plays. That there was a coalition between the folk-play and the developing popular drama of the 14th and 15th centuries is an attractive theory; E. K. Chambers's *The English Folk-Play*, first published in 1933, provides plenty of evidence. However, the problem is one for the folklorist to examine rather than for the literary critic, whose judgment has to depend on written records and texts. The critic must assume a remote pre-literary source for many features of the Mummers' Play, such as the combat, the presence of the healing Doctor and the revival from death in battle, all of which make their appearance in both religious and secular drama of the 15th century.

TOURNAMENT

Another link with mediæval and Renaissance drama seems to have been the tournament, which was popular with an audience that enjoyed spectacle. Tournament provided tension between two opposing sides, and the fascination of individual hand-to-hand combat between champions. It was a training for war, dangerous to life and limb. In 1179 Pope Alexander III threatened to deny burial rights to those killed, and other popes tried to excommunicate participants. They were officially banned in England until the accession of Richard I in 1189. He encouraged them as a uniting influence, associated them with high ideals and festivities and made them popular with his discontented barons. Under the influence of the knightly code of chivalry, the cruder mock-battle of the 11th and 12th centuries was gradually refined into what amounted to an art of combat, and the tournament, which signified a passage-of-arms between troops, was succeeded by the joust, or single combat, with the lists, the watching ladies betting on their favourites and the heroics which inspired Sir Walter Scott to write *Ivanhoe* and *The Talisman*.

In the 14th century women began to influence the proceedings, and formal etiquette began to play its part so that a fabric of allegory enveloped the knight taking part in mock-combat. He was encouraged to take his role seriously, like a hero going to his death. This may not have been an exaggeration, since a fall from a charging horse when clad in armour weighing about sixty pounds could easily break a man's back. In preparation for his ordeal the knight, who had spent about half his lifetime studying martial skills, went through a complicated ritual of dedication, self-immolation and covenanting with death, akin to the ceremonies undergone by Japanese *Kamikaze* pilots towards the end of the Second World War. The discovery of gunpowder made armour obsolete in actual battle, and the tournament became more and more of an entertainment. By 1500, deaths and serious injuries were rare, and although the joust on foot was still practised in Shakespeare's time, it had become stylised. Under the Puritans it died out altogether.

Apart from the elaborate chivalric paraphernalia, the interest of the tournament lay in its colourfulness, elaborate costuming, which helped combatants and spectators to separate friend from foe, and the many displays of coats-of-arms, crests, plumes and blazonry in the primary colours. The tournament profoundly affected the popular imagination of the mediæval Englishman, for although participation in the combats was reserved for gentlemen, admission as a spectator was not, and the festivities belonged almost as much to the populace as to the aristocracy. To read a description of a tournament is to learn a good deal about the kind of spectacle which a mediæval audience liked, and it may explain to some extent why popular playwrights inserted so many highly-coloured scenes of violent action having but an indirect connection with their main plot.

PAGEANT

Bearing a similar relationship to the development of drama is the pageant, which flourished in England from the early part of the 13th century. A pageant was primarily public celebration of, for example, a military victory, or was designed to emphasise the appearance of a ruler before his subjects, or, more lavishly, to mark a coronation or a royal wedding. These demonstrations took place in the streets of London and the larger towns and were organised by the municipal trade guilds with the assistance of the church authorities in much the same way as the miracle play cycles, with which the pageants had much in common. The unity of a pageant was founded in a still-life symbol of a theme, not in a plot or a character, and the person to be honoured by the pageant appeared before a number of successive stages. On each stage a scene was arranged and the whole series made up a tableau. The effect seems to have been rather like that of a gallery of pictures, and the audience consisted not only of the honoured guest himself, together with his retinue, moving in procession from one stage to the next, but also of the public at large, forgathered to see the procession. Guests accompanying the retinue, hosts and townsfolk were thus united as integral parts of the spectacle which they themselves had come to witness. Because of their symbolic character, the spectators in course of time came to know what to look for in presentations of this 'dumb poesie'. We have records of pageants in London, Worcester, York, Bristol, Coventry and other cities, and Professor Wickham gives a very full account of them in *Early English Stages*; some were religious but more often than not their aim was political, and they tried to emphasise a moral of government or depict a theme correcting injustice. Towards the end of the

14th century speech was introduced to reinforce mime so that we have the pompous rhetorical declamation, accompanied by music and the singing of anthems, such as marked the coronation of Richard II in 1377.

In these tableaux, the characters of folk-plays stand side by side with those of history and scriptural tradition, conventionally attired, so that the audiences could interpret their significance. St. George is accompanied by the Dragon; the King, often identifiable as an actual monarch of England, is crowned; his cloak is purple or crimson and he bears an orb or a sceptre. As in the *Prophetae*, the Saints are identifiable by what they carry. Peter holds the keys of the Kingdom of Heaven, Christopher is accompanied by a child, and Simon, Thomas and Paul grasp a saw, a lance and a sword respectively, signifying the instruments of their martyrdom. The human symbols of religious art which appear in mosaics of Christian churches as early as the 4th century were used consistently and continuously in paintings and cathedral windows throughout the Middle Ages, until living actors finally lent reality to them as named personages in miracle play and pageant.

The trend was inevitably towards a wider choice of subject, and secular figures soon began to dominate the tableaux. The Seven Deadly Sins and the stock Virtues and Vices, such as Justice with her naked sword, Truth and her book, Hypocrisy with her cloak and the tattered figures of Poverty and his attendant Misery, were joined early in the 16th century by the Seven Liberal Sciences, and characters from newly-rediscovered classical learning, such as Jason, Apollo and Paris. The pageant represents the formal development present in English drama from its beginnings, and the influence of the fixed stages on the early morality plays is clearly perceptible in *The Castell of Perseverance*, composed about 1420, designed for a fixed stage and depending largely on speaking tableaux. Sir David Lyndsay's *Ane Satyre of the Thrie Estaitis*, first performed about 1530, is a late mediæval morality play which presents the three Estates, Church, State and Commons, in powerfully symbolic terms, and preaches a political sermon in a series of episodes, peopled by familiar allegorical figures, like those of pageant, but far more lively and individual. Shakespeare felt the influence of pageants, and may indeed have written for this 'theatre of the streets', as did his contemporaries, Jonson, Dekker and Heywood. The effects of spectacle and ceremonial parade are prominent features of several of Shakespeare's historical and Roman plays. In *Antony and Cleopatra*, for example, the military grandeur of imperial Rome is set against the beguiling attractions of ancient Egypt by means of a succession of contrasting scenes composed with an eye to the colourful and the spacious.

If the rustic rituals, the colourful tournaments and the 'dumb poesie' of the pageants were combined with the liturgical drama of the Christian Church, the result would be close to an English miracle play. The play cycles are the first specifically English, as distinct from European, drama. The Passion plays which we know to have been performed in the south of England have been lost, so that the extant miracles have, by their survival, attained a greater stature than might have been the case otherwise. They were written in English, not Latin or French, and were under the direction of laity, not clergy. In them we may see what happened to the religious drama when it was touched by the English spirit of comedy.

VESTIGES OF CLASSICAL DRAMA

In spite of all our extensive researches and hypotheses we still do not know how drama originated. The Greeks found its origin in the dance, by which they meant rhythmical movement of any kind. The mimetic rituals of agricultural communities in which they imitated the processes of the season's work are, as we have noted, usually grounded in dancing; and for both the Greeks and the Romans there seems to have been little distinction between solemnity and indecorousness in such ritual celebrations. Roman circus performances, gladiatorial combats and all the varied activities of the hippodrome were conducted in an atmosphere of unrestrained exhibitionism. All these could be described as *ludi*. The drama was only one such activity and, because of its dubious associations, never occupied a respected place in Roman leisure occupations. Livy calls these low farces *saturæ* or 'medleys', perhaps because they were essentially formless and lacked any definite plot. They seem to have been a mixture of dialogue and song, and as time went on, these productions, called *mimi* or *pantomimi*, degenerated. The Church was an old enemy of the stage. As early as the 2nd century Tertullian had attacked *ludi* in his treatise *De Spectaculis*, saying even of the best of them that 'the moral good induced was only a drop of honey, mixed with the poison of toads'. Statements of the same kind were current until the 17th century.

The despised mimes and pantomimes of the disintegrating Roman Empire seem to have gone underground, for after the Church frowned on them officially, we hear of them no more though they must have continued in private performance before being absorbed into the repertoires of itinerant entertainers. These minstrels, acrobats, jugglers, conjurors, wrestlers, dancers and animal-trainers, travelling singly or in troupes, earning their bread by amusing the people, must have included some endowed with the talents appropriate to an actor, who could render monologues or duologues in costume with the help of elementary properties. Such reciters, of the type of the Germanic *scop* or glee-man, must have brought welcome variety to the peasant enduring his humdrum existence throughout those long winters.

ANGLO-SAXON NARRATIVE POEMS

From their content and style it is evident that most of the Old English poems were designed for dramatic recitation. A stirring epic like *The Battle of Maldon*, which tells of an actual clash of arms between the English and the Danes in 991, could not have been delivered other than dramatically and it was almost certainly composed for an audience who wanted more than straightforward recitation. The poem is studded with passages describing battle, the clang of sword against shield and the bold boastings of Byrhtwold and the diminishing survivors of Byrhtnoth's stalwart fighting men as they stood their ground before a superior force of attackers:

Then Byrhtnoth drew the sword from the sheath, broad and gleaming-edged, and struck at the corslet. One of the seafarers got in his way too quickly and wounded the earl in the arm. Then the sword with its golden hilt fell down to the ground.

'Resolve shall be the harder, heart the keener, courage the greater, as our might lessens. Here lies our leader, all hewn down, the valiant man in the dust. May he lament for ever who thinks now to turn from this war-play. I am old in age; I will not hence, but I purpose to lie by the side of my lord, by the man so dearly loved.'

Earlier alliterative poems, like *The Dream of the Rood*, composed about A.D. 800, essentially a dramatic monologue supposedly uttered by the Cross on which Christ was crucified, or *Beowulf*, the greatest of the works left by the Anglo-Saxons, both invite an actor's delivery. *The Dream of the Rood* is the more subtle poem, demanding interpretation from its reader and depending for its effects on tone of voice, rise and fall of syllables and the capacity of the speaker to recreate a mood, or rather a series of moods, for though this poem is short, it ripples constantly.

Lo! I will declare the best of dreams which I dreamt in the middle of the night, when human creatures lay at rest. It seemed to me that I saw a wondrous tree rising aloft, encompassed with light, the brightest of crosses. . . . It was long ago—I still remember it— that I was cut down at the edge of the forest, moved from my trunk. Strong enemies took me there, till they set me on a hill; many foes made me fast there. . . . Then the young Hero—he was God Almighty—firm and unflinching, stripped Himself; He mounted on the high cross, brave in the sight of many. . . . As a rood was I raised up; I bore aloft the mighty King, the Lord of heaven; I dared not stoop. They pierced me with dark nails; the wounds are still plain to view in me, gaping gashes of malice. . . . Cold grew the corpse, fair house of the Soul. . . . On me the Son of God suffered for a space; wherefore now I rise glorious beneath the heavens and I can heal all who fear me.

The first known English poem, the Caedmon *Hymn of the Creation*, dating from about 680, is a song of action celebrating the creation of the world, the very stuff of drama.

Now we must praise the Guardian of the Kingdom of Heaven, the Creator's power and his forethought; the work of the Father of Glory as he, eternal lord, established in the beginning each marvel. He first created for the children of earth Heaven for a roof, the Holy Creator; the guardian of mankind, the eternal lord, the Almighty God, afterwards created the World, the Earth, for men.

These phrases sound much more magnificent in the West-Saxon version:

Nū sculon herigean	heofonrīces Weard
Meotodes meahte	ond his mōdgeþanc
weorc Wuldorfæder;	swā hē wundra gehwæs,
ēce Drihten,	ōr onstealde.
Hē ǣrest sceōp	eorðan bearnum
heofon tō hrōfe,	hālig Scyppend;
Þa middangeard,	moncynnes Weard,
ēce Drihten,	æfter tēode
fīrum foldan,	Frēa ælmihtig.

Sweet's *AS Reader*, revised D. Whitelock, O.U.P., 1967 (15th ed.)

This poem is a piece made up of 'gesture-words', to be emphasised by sweeping movements of the arms, conveying vastness, omniscience and the terrible wonder of the divine power. After the Norman Conquest, certain Christian poems, such as *Poema Morale*, *Cursor Mundi* and the *Judas* fragment, gave scope to monologuists, and it is evident from the alliterative style and lyrical forms of Old and Early Middle English poetry that the dramatic element is fundamental. It was composed for oral recitation and the strain of argument, injunction, exhortation and conversation is strong in it, even when the poem in question is not cast in the form of a debate or questioning narrative, as many of them were. *The Owl and the Nightingale*, which reflects the antagonism between asceticism and gay pleasures, or *Wynnere and Wastour*, wherein the spendthrift and the squanderer argue as to which of the two is acting the more wisely, are both formal debates open to dramatic representation. When we come to Chaucer, it is easy to see certain of his works, for example *The Parlement of Foules* or *The Nun's Priest's Tale*, as creations by a narrator strongly influenced by the idea of men and women playing parts; he puts in their mouths convincing dialogue which would sound very well on a stage. The powerful tradition of mediæval preaching was, in any case, at the service of contemporary acting, for the techniques of the skilled pulpit orator, the mendicant friar of the 13th and 14th centuries expounding the Gospel, equipped with a colourful vocabulary, a battery of anecdotes and a range of histrionic gestures, and who knew what his audience wanted, were precisely those of the trained character-actor. Chaucer's Pardoner, though a charlatan and a conscious hypocrite, is just such an actor.

No contemporary preacher ever mentions the plays except in a contemptuous tone or in carefully-restricted terms of approval, but it is undoubtedly true that the pulpit was the principal medium of instruction in the sacred mysteries, and indeed had been so for 300 years. In homiletic sources like *Cursor Mundi* or *Legenda Aurea* the mediæval preacher found the material which he embellished with all the rhetorical aids that his natural ability could learn to manipulate; in fact, there is no expression in the miracle cycles, satiric, tragic, pathetic or naïvely comic, that does not have its previous counterpart and possible inspiration in a sermon-collection. Popular preaching was the link between the liturgical play and the town-cycles, and we should look to the itinerant friars, talking not in Latin but in vernacular English, for the 'efficient cause' of the native development and popular dissemination of the drama.

FORMAL CLASSICAL DRAMA

But what became of the formal classical drama? Historians of the theatre have stated that after the Church passed its edict, the play as we know it died out until about the year 1100, except for the religious ritual which provided a substitute. How true is this?

In the first place, it is not true to say that formal drama ceased to exist. Plays were written. What is less certain is whether any of them were ever performed in the presence of an audience. Greek dramatic traditions survived vestigially in Eastern Europe but not significantly in the West. Seneca and Plautus were frequently quoted as authorities but did not exert a perceptible influence on the theatre until the Renaissance. Terence, perhaps because his style was thought suitable for imitation by the young, survived as a text-book model of lucid writing, and in the 10th century the Saxon nun Hrostwitha of Gandersheim wrote six plays in rhymed Latin prose avowedly under Terentian influence. These do not seem to have been acted except, possibly, in the chapter-house for the benefit of the enclosed nuns and the princesses of the Saxon court who directed the convent, known at the time as an intellectual centre. As mirrored in her plays, Hrostwitha is an exceptionally interesting personality and calls for attention in spite of her historical remoteness and lack of influence.

Hrostwitha did not enter the Gandersheim convent until she was twenty-five, which might explain the worldly wisdom of her plays, which in some respects anticipate those of Calderon, Lope de Vega and the Elizabethan comedies. *Callimachus and Drusina* contains snatches of dialogue which suggest Romeo's approaches to Juliet. Here is one, rendered from the Latin:

D.: What makes you love me?
C.: Your beauty.
D.: My beauty?
C.: That's right.
D.: And what has it to do with you?
C.: At this moment, nothing, unfortunately, but I hope, one day . . .

and later Callimachus weeps on Drusina's tomb, as Romeo does on Juliet's.

Even more remarkable for its time is Hrostwitha's *Abraham*, a play with a solid plot in which Abraham, an old hermit of the desert, goes into a brothel to retrieve his niece whom ill-fortune had forced there. Abraham poses as a client, and when the ladies of the house are brought in for his inspection, chooses his niece from among them and, by this ruse, manages to extricate her from her predicament. The pair make their way out of the place and Abraham leads the girl back across the desert. The desert is a stock symbol of life and Abraham of the ascetic guide, but the play's Christian significance is less to be noted than is the lifelike dialogue in the scenes within the brothel. All Hrostwitha's dramatic pieces extol virginity, and in this respect are antithetical to Terence's, though there is assuredly nothing cloistered about her depiction of human nature. Hrostwitha died about 1002, but the plays were lost until about 1500 and cannot be said to have had any impact on the European secular theatre.

Terence, and more directly Ovid, also provided inspiration for a number of elegiac comedies produced between 1000 and 1200. Mediæval comedy was a form of narrative in colloquial speech, dealing with society's lower ranks and proceeding from misfortune to a happy ending. Tragedy was held to be a tale in which prosperity was succeeded by misery, not necessarily brought about by any fault on the part of the tragic figures themselves—Fortune or Fate governed the affairs of men, who were not individually responsible for what happened to them. Chaucer's *Monk's Tale*, suggested by Boccaccio's *De Casibus Virorum Illustrium*, consisted of a series of short accounts dealing with the misfortunes of great men. Some, like Nero, deserved what Fate had in store for them, others, like Samson, brought about their own destruction, but others again, like the two children of Hugolino, Count of Pisa, who, with their father, starved to death in captivity, were the helpless victims of ill-luck. Hrostwitha's 'comedies' are not funny; although they include comic scenes the dominant impression is what we should call tragi-comic, for there is a masterly portrayal of suffering in a play like *Dulcitius*, which is about an official whose attempts to deflower three holy virgins are frustrated by divine forces. Dante's *Divine Comedy*, the greatest work of the Middle Ages, is also the most serious in overall temper, but, written in the vernacular, it fulfilled commonly-held notions of what *comedia* ought to be.

These elegiac comedies, however, were not serious in temper. There were over twenty of them, either short, dramatic narratives or, in two cases, plays capable of being acted. One of the latter deserves mention since it circulated widely in manuscript form and, with the advent of printing, ran to sixteen editions from 1470 onwards. This was the 12th-century *Pamphilus seu de*

Amore, a Latin play dealing with a stock classical theme, seduction, in the spirit of Ovid's *Ars Amatoria*. The popularity of the work was such that it was soon translated into French, under the title of *Pamphile et Galatée*, by Jean Brasdefer in 1225. (From its title the English language derives the word 'pamphlet'.) There is no record of its having been acted, but it is the only elegiac comedy to achieve long-lasting fame, and this in itself suggests performance rather than recitation. However, like the others, its direct influence on the development of secular drama is hard to estimate, for its Ovidian cynicism was soon afterwards to be reflected in the more influential *Roman de la Rose* which inspired Chaucer and others to compose dream-visions. *Pamphilus* has the same four characters as *Le Roman*, the young man and woman, the goddess of love, and the old woman. Anus, the old woman, is a precursor of the Wife of Bath and a host of other female deceivers who agree that men should be cheated if possible, that it is not difficult to do so because they are all so conceited, and that all women desire freedom to fulfil their sexual life as they please. She is the first of a series of fictitious ladies in French, Italian, Spanish and English literature who reveal feminine character through talk and whose descent may be traced back to Ovid, of whose cynical view of love they are lifelike symbols.

Generally speaking, therefore, the formal classical dramatic writing of the Middle Ages consisted in a following of models. It had no connection with the religious drama and so far as we know, it was a cloistered amusement which, rarely if ever performed, had little or nothing to do with the living stage. The stage was 'popular', and when the nature of mediæval English drama is considered, one thinks first and foremost of the miracle play cycles in which for the first and probably the last time, the play and the people came together to associate in a common purpose.

4

Miracle Plays

The English miracle plays were grouped in cycles connected with a central idea, Redemption, expressed through familiar biblical themes. There were several reasons why such cycles evolved. One factor influencing the style of production was weather; the English climate has never been reliable and since there were no theatres, performances had to be presented in the open air at a time of year when the weather was most likely to be dry and warm. Whitsuntide, six weeks after Easter, was a favourite period, but the day which became most prominent as a time of procession and public entertainment was that of the High Feast of Corpus Christi. Pope Urban VI first sanctioned the Feast in 1264, half a century after the Fourth Lateran Council had approved the doctrine of transubstantiation. First popular in Belgium, it was officially observed in England in June 1311. Its characteristic feature is a colourful procession in which the Host, or consecrated bread, is carried on a circuit of the streets. It is still commemorated in European countries, including France, Germany, Switzerland, Italy, Spain and Portugal, on the Thursday following Trinity Sunday, fifty-seven days after Easter. Here is a present-day account of the Festival:

> In the city of Ponta Delgada, on San Miguel, on Corpus Christi Sunday the inhabitants make a magnificent flower-petal carpet—almost three-quarters of a mile in length—over which the procession passes. High-ranking clergy wearing gorgeous vestments and walking under an embroidered canopy, are accompanied by acolytes who swing censers and hold tall white candles. Hundreds of red-robed priests follow, then a charming group of first

communicants—little boys in dark suits and scarlet capes and little girls in white frocks and filmy veils.

The climax of the ceremony comes when the bishop, in vestments woven with gold and silver thread, slowly raises the silver monstrance and exposes the Blessed Sacrament, symbol of the Body of Christ. Worshippers sink to their knees. As if to enhance the solemnity of the moment, the setting sun often drenches the bowed heads of the vast throng with warm glowing light.

D. G. Spicer, FESTIVALS OF WESTERN EUROPE

This mediæval Feast is a symbol of the pure heart, prepared by contrition and confession to receive the Body and Blood of Christ. The procession and the ambulatory drama which accompanied it in mediæval England had as its purpose the sanctification of the secular, as Professor Wickham puts it: 'an attempt, inspired by the example of the Friars, to inject the very liturgy itself into the environment of daily living'.

A description of the York Corpus Christi procession is given in *Collectanea Bradfordiana*, printed in Volume I of *British Calendar Customs*; unlike present-day accounts, it emphasises the plays:

On the day before and on the morning of the day itself, thousands of spectators streamed into the city. On Corpus Christi morn, artisans and tradesmen rose early, spending an hour or two completing the arrangements of their large stages. At 9 a.m. the procession started, beginning to play first at the gates of the priory of the Holy Trinity in Micklegate; then it proceeded to every street and so every street had a pageant 'all at one time playing together'. Scaffolds and stages were erected in the street in those places where they determined to play their pageants. On the route, the procession reached the cathedral and, on leaving it, went on through Girdler Gate and across the Pavement to All Hallows Church, the actors playing, all the time, their Mystery Plays bearing titles such as, for example, Cain and Abel, Slaughter of the Innocents, and Deliverance of Souls from Hell.

In the year 1415, fifty-four distinct dramas were represented on fifty-four stages, some of which were arranged upon scaffolds capable of carrying a great weight. Among the subjects selected were The Creation, Murder of Abel, Adam and Eve, The Brazen

Serpent, Abraham and Isaac, Slaughter of the Innocents, and the Last Judgment. Fifty-six actors were required for one pageant, forty-three for a second, and thirty-four for a third; few plays required not less than ten actors. The total number of actors would not be less than 700. There were fifty-eight citizens bearing torches, thirty-seven civic officers and their attendants, and a great number of duly habited priests. The total number of persons assisting in the ceremonies was not less than a thousand.

The scaffolds, elaborately furnished stages, mechanical appliances, dresses richly adorned, gold and silver lace, silver buckles and chains, embroidered fabrics, animals of various kinds, representations of clouds, a fiercely burning hell, and a representation of the world on fire, suggest a list of necessaries provided regardless of cost.

The Corpus Christi plays were kept up till the year 1584, at York.

This is probably based on later rather than earlier accounts of the manner of performing the plays, since most 15th-century references to properties suggest that they were simple. The perfection of gadgets and 'theatre engines' is associated more with Leonardo da Vinci and Brunelleschi in Florence than with the English stage-designers of York. An 1825 volume called *A Dissertation on the Pageants or Dramatic Mysteries anciently performed at Coventry by the Trading Companies of that City; chiefly with reference to the Vehicle, Characters, and Dresses of the Actors*, by the antiquary Thomas Sharp, contains a plate showing a stage, actors and spectators, and plates with representations of Hell, either as a burning crater or as a large open-topped furnace, with bellows and tools for stoking. The height of the stage and supporting vehicle together is apparently about fifteen feet. Again there is a suggestion of a greater realism than the usual painted hell-mouth would convey, so that it is likely that the passage of time encouraged the producers to develop visual effects which, for a play on the Last Judgment, might have been considered essential—the smoke and flames of the inferno. Such a scene must have been a strong aid to Repentance. After the Reformation the Festival was abolished in England, but its survival in Catholic Europe helps one to imagine the nature of

63

the carnival spirit which it encouraged in towns where miracle cycles came to be regularly performed (see cover).

When performances began is not known. Documentary evidence of miracles given before 1375 is lacking. F. M. Salter points out in his *Mediæval Drama in Chester* that

> There are no plays surviving in England, which, linguistically or otherwise, show any traces of greater antiquity than the last quarter of the fourteenth century; and there are no firm references to mysteries at any earlier date.

This statement has to be balanced against contemporary references to presentations of the cycles as of ancient custom. It is not impossible, therefore, that the cyclic performance of plays had been established in 1328, as 16th-century tradition suggests. The cycles and many of the individual plays are of composite authorship, and the complete building-up of a cycle took many years, probably fifty to sixty. The contribution of the Wakefield Master, of whom we shall speak presently, has been dated in the 1430s, whereas much of the material in this cycle is revised from the plays of York, which were being performed in 1378. Moreover, although there were at least a dozen cycles, only four have been handed down to us in their entirety, together with four other single plays and one fragment which once were part of whole cycles. Most of the scriptural drama of the 14th and 15th centuries has been lost or destroyed, since records testify to the existence of many other cycles. E. K. Chambers compiled a list, indicating that scriptural plays were presented in nearly every populated region of England and a great many in Scotland as well, since many borough records mention performances from 1450 onwards. Like the manuscripts of Old English poetry and prose, what has been preserved has survived by luck, and except for the Chester cycle, which exists in five texts, one York play and the Norwich play of the Creation, in two versions, only unique manuscripts remain to us. The town authorities possessed a single complete copy of a cycle, and the trade guild responsible for producing a play within that cycle might possess a copy of that play alone. In fact only one of the guild copies survives, from the York cycle—guilds as well as towns guarded their plays jealously, as part of their *mystique*: they felt that a certain play 'belonged' to a particular guild and was in that respect private property.

In probable order of establishment, then, the first of the four cycles is the Chester, dated *c.* 1375, with twenty-four plays, narrative and lyrical in character, and lacking in some of the more ear- or eye-catching techniques of the other cycles. The York cycle was in existence, though in an early form, in 1378, with forty-eight plays, the work of at least three shadowy authors, of whom two are called the 'metrist' and the 'realist'. There is a second Yorkshire cycle of thirty-two plays, apparently a revision of the first, known as the Towneley cycle after the name of the owner of the manuscript, a 19th-century Lancashire squire. This is more accurately called the Wakefield cycle. The main interest of this series is that it contains the plays of a markedly individual contributor called 'the Wakefield Master', who flourished about 1430. The last of the four cycles is the heavily theological N-town or Hegge cycle, better known as the *Ludus Coventriae*, composed of forty-two plays. The 'N-town' comes from the banns introducing the plays:

A sunday next yf that we may
At vi of the belle we gin oure play
In N-towne.

'N' may stand for *Nomen* or name, suggesting a blank to be filled in by the crier proclaiming the banns. It is certainly not Coventry, of which the cycle, except for two plays, is lost, and a strong case has been advanced, by Professor Hardin Craig in *English Religious Drama of the Middle Ages*, for Lincoln. To avoid confusion, we shall refer to it as the N-town cycle. One play each remains to us from the Norwich and the Newcastle-on-Tyne cycles, in even later transcripts—one of the 17th, the second of the 18th centuries. In addition there are several single plays which may or may not have been part of cycles, e.g. the Digby *Slaughter of the Innocents*, transcribed about 1512, and two plays of Abraham and Isaac: the Brome play, which is late 15th century and is based on the Chester play on the same subject, and a Dublin Abraham play, probably originally from Northampton and dating from about 1458. Both the Brome and the Dublin plays have been highly praised by critics for their emotional qualities.

These are all that survive of the miracle plays proper. One may add a Cornish trilogy, composed of *The Origin of the World*, *The Passion of Our Lord* and *The Resurrection*, dramatising several legends not found in English cycles; but these were in Cornish, a local language not spoken after the 17th century. By most modern scholars, all these plays are known as 'miracle', which is in fact a Middle English and Old French word, more common on the Continent than in England and originally applied to saints' plays only. A play on a Bible subject was called *Mystère*, and to add to the confusion this term was also in use by 1375 to describe the occupation of a member of a trade guild—we still refer to the 'mysteries' of a craft, meaning the skills attached to that craft or the initiation rites for new entrants which together serve to preserve the uniqueness of the craft society. There is in addition the term 'pageant', which may point either at an individual play within a cycle or to the wheeled waggon on which the play was performed. Unfortunately there does not seem to be a complete agreement among critics and scholars on the use of these terms. In view of this it is perhaps best to call all English scriptural plays 'miracles' and qualify 'pageant' with 'waggon' when the movable stage is meant.

THE GUILDS

Each of the craft guilds had its patron saint and was in character semi-religious, dedicated to uphold the Corpus Christi Feast and its function as a symbol of the Redeemer, so that it was an inevitable step, as plays grew more involved, for the guilds to take them over. What could not be performed in the interior of a church found a more appropriate location immediately outside; non-Gospel characters, merchants, devils, drunken servants and the dozens of minor personages added to give the play realism could be more appropriately played by laymen than by priests. Larger casts and greater expenses and the popular didactic function of the miracles made their direction by the secular fellowships a necessary development.

What were these guilds? All were of religious origin and character, but most were linked to a specific trade or craft. They were well established in the 14th century and had developed civic functions, even to the extent of running local government. Their closest counterpart today is the Benefit or Provident Society, for they represented a strong sense of municipal loyalty, built schools, hospitals and churches, and in a like spirit took over control of the miracle play cycles. Members of the trade guilds, the master-craftsmen, included men of refined tastes who represented the best of the new bourgeois class which came into prominence in the late Middle Ages. The capitalist strivings of the *nouveaux riches* were despised by nobles and clergy, and both Chaucer and Langland indulged in many a dig at their expense, but in the long run these people represented a civilising influence on mediæval society, demanded a higher standard of education for their children, and over two or three generations became patrons of the arts. At least, this was certainly the case in northern Europe, and though in England its members were far less voracious in the acquisition of wealth and property than were their European counterparts, this new mercantile class enhanced the land, grew powerful and became a force to be reckoned with in government. The mediæval rhyme:

God hath shapen lyves thre
Boor and kniȝt and prest they be

summed up an attitude to life which by Chaucer's time had been heavily undermined.

As business expanded, the guilds proliferated. Each craft had its own guild; the textile industry, a very important one at that time since it was the spearhead of the new prosperity in England, included guilds for wool-combers, spinners, two kinds of silk-spinner, seven kinds of weaver, dyers, fullers, calenders, shearmen, sellers and four kinds of tailor. The guilds exercised ruthless monopolies and no townsmen could engage in a given craft unless he were enrolled in the appropriate guild. The markets sold only the products of guild members and there were stiff regulations for apprenticeship, requiring a period of training ranging from two to ten years, depending on the craft—the goldsmiths, for example, demanded ten years. The successful apprentice became a journeyman, but although he earned a wage he could work only for a master. To become a master he had to pass a test by making a 'masterpiece'. Only then could he set himself up on his own and employ apprentices, but he was always under the strict regulation of the guild, which insisted on superlative craftsmanship, and denied its 'hallmark' or guildhall seal of approval to shoddy articles. The guilds kept up their standards by means of pressure from inspectors and the threat of expulsion. Strict regulations concerning hours of work, price levels, and forbidding advertising were inspired by the Church, which preached that the profit motive was an ignoble one, and in this way a *mystique* developed. The power of the guilds was represented by aldermen, elected annually from each guild, who formed the city council, headed by a mayor. The guilds were closed circles so far as the general public was concerned, but they existed to keep standards high and to protect the ordinary man against the rapscallions of trade. Of course, their regulations were flouted by 'rugged individualists' who wanted to make profit over the heads of the guilds; but on the whole these ancient companies seem to have managed to maintain their aloofness from the cruder aspects of mercantile competition and continued to take their self-imposed obligations seriously. In fact, they applied the Christian principle of *caritas* to trade.

These, then, were the organisations which, with Church support, assumed the responsibility for staging the miracle play cycles in connection with religious processions like the Corpus Christi Feast, and later, in the 15th century, with fairs such as the Lammas or St. Peter's Fair, performed during the Vigil of the Feast of St. Peter. In York there were over fifty guilds, each with its own church.

The municipal officers, the representatives of the guilds, exercised a strict control over every aspect of the performance—this is especially apparent in the documents of the City of York, which are more detailed than any others. The York cycle is the most complete, and exists in one manuscript, the Ashburnham, dating from about 1450. As noted previously, there seem to have been three authors, living at three different periods; of these the first may have been a monk of the same St. Mary's Abbey where the modern performances are held. The regulating hand of one individual is clearly seen throughout the series, however.

The excitement attending a production of the cycle must have been very great, since it occurred only once a year, and was announced with great ceremony by the town crier reading 'banns'. Although the York cycle could be completed in one day, it had to start at 4.30 a.m. and did not stop until dusk—at that time of year 9.30 p.m., so that the Mercers' play of the Judgment with its rather tedious declamations must have been played in half-light or by the aid of some elementary illumination such as is mentioned in the York manuscript. Though it had only half as many plays, the Chester cycle was spread over three days. Therefore it seems to be a practical impossibility that the entire series of thirty-two Wakefield plays, accompanied by the Corpus Christi procession, could have been played in one day. In 1426, it is recorded, the procession took place on the day *after* the performance of the York cycle, and a similar separation occurred at Chester and at Norwich and, much later, at Wakefield. This spreading-over of the time allotted for the playing of the cycle is understandable, but it does seem likely that earlier performances demanded a Herculean effort from both players and audience so that the whole spectacle, including the procession, could be staged in a day. When Queen Margaret attended a performance at Coventry in 1457 she witnessed the entire cycle except the *Doomsday Play*, which was not performed because there was not enough daylight. It is reasonable to assume that some reliable means of getting through the performances, by making cuts or by telescoping, was usually adopted.

The processional street-pageant staging of the York cycle, wherein the plays were performed at a number of different places in the city, was traditionally supposed to permit the entire cycle to be produced at each station in turn. We know that there were from twelve to sixteen stations at York, and that in 1554 fifty-seven plays were staged at sixteen different stations. It is possible that acting of the plays took place in one locality only, and that 'stations' marked the various points at which tableaux of each of the plays were set up to be visited in turn by the procession *before* the actual speaking of the lines began. The instruction in the York proclamation telling all the players to be in their positions by 4.30 a.m. makes very little sense unless it refers to the staging of tableaux, since the cast of the Judgment play, performed last, would surely have no other reason to turn out at dawn.

The N-town plays (probably the Lincoln plays) were acted not in a series of pageants in procession, but on a standing group of pageant-waggons arranged round a central area called 'the place'—the reverse, in fact, of the modern theatre in the round. Vivid stage directions give a graphic picture of the manner of performance, and the cycle thus illustrates important advances in stage technique. The plays were acted by one guild, not a craft guild but a religious one called the St. Anne Guild, which included as members every man and woman in Lincoln. After 1470 the Corpus Christi procession took place on St. Anne's Day, 26th July. According to Professor Hardin Craig, there was a procession of waggons which wended its way to the cathedral, where the plays were performed on one playing-site within the cathedral close. Spectators viewed them from scaffolds or stands, and the pageant-waggons themselves were arranged in a semi-circle. There was thus a large circular area marked by spectators' stands and waggons.

The N-town plays, the Digby plays and the missing Norwich cycle, all of which were the responsibility of religious and not trade guilds, were all performed in one fixed locality; we know from various municipal records that performances in Scotland at Aberdeen and Edinburgh and many stagings in smaller English towns were presented in this way. It was only in York and Chester that processional pageants seem to have been the practice; the Wakefield plays, which resemble the N-town cycle in that both are compilations of Old and New Testament plays organised as a continuous sequence and showing a clear attempt at overall design, were evidently intended for fixed performance. In this cycle there are 243 parts, and in the town of Wakefield in the year 1377, there were under 300 men over sixteen. Only a handful of these were craftsmen, which suggests that the cycle was associated with a larger group—even then, the doubling of parts would have been unavoidable. Dramatically, of course, this made for greater continuity, and encouraged individual interpretations of characters like Jesus, Herod and Pilate, who appeared in a number of plays. In the York cycle, on the other hand, there were twenty-seven plays having Jesus as a character and, under the *aegis* of the trade guilds, this meant that twenty-seven different members of the guilds played the part of Jesus. The desire for continuity of actors necessitated by a shortage of available talent made performance in a fixed locality practically unavoidable. This strengthens the impression that the Wakefield cycle, like most of the others, was performed in one location. Stage directions for this cycle require two acting areas, and there are several plays, such as the *Second Shepherds' Play*, where this is obvious, for Mak's cottage and the manger have to be clearly represented. In the stage directions these areas are called 'mansions', and sometimes, as in *The Offering of the Magi*, the three actors playing the parts of the kings are required to ride horses into the acting area from different directions and even to ride between 'mansions'. The Wakefield Passion sequence could only achieve continuity through scene-changes, and would require a minimum of four separate pageant-stages, widely spaced. There are many plays where the acting could only have been successful on multiple stages in a fixed location.

Sometimes performance must have been 'in the round', as in the N-town cycle. In the manuscript there are two entries directing that pageants be moved into 'the place', and in the Wakefield *Noah*, in which Noah has to build his Ark in full view of the audience while giving a running commentary on his work, stage directions demand the drawing into 'the place' of the Ark on wheels. In plays where different elevations, such as Heaven and Hell, or a position of greater height from which God may address Cain or Abraham, are required, one- or two-tiered pageant-waggons, connected to the ground level by means of ladders, and a central acting area are implied and sometimes actually prescribed in the stage directions. By the mid-15th century producers' methods had advanced very considerably, and one may be sure that there were some extremely fertile minds at work behind the scenes of these plays, adapting properties to situations and situations to properties with every bit as much imagination and skill as their present-day counterparts. Contemporary stage directions seem to have been governed by a desire to achieve a continuity of dramatic action previously lacking, so that sequences were given a unity and an increased pace which must have had the result of heightening the effect of realism.

To sum up, then, it is likely that the most common method of staging miracle plays was not in a series of pageants but at fixed booths representing different localities, so that as the scenes changed the actors could move from one to another by passing through the watching crowd. Parts of the plays were acted on the ground before the fixed stages, and from a brightly-painted hell-mouth issued devils who might have drawn the spectators into the action by seizing or otherwise annoying them. The minor imps were invariably made into comic figures and were the ancestors of the stage Vice of the moralities, and eventually of the Elizabethan clown. Their humour was rough and melodramatic, largely improvised for the occasion, and a good deal of their effect had its source in their grisly costumes—a challenge to the ingenuity of the individual actors, who made themselves look as fiercely ridiculous as they could, sooty, with long noses, deformed extra limbs, reptilian wings and distorted visages. The gargoyles on mediæval buildings or the pagan demons in

Death uses the monarch's crown as a rest, thus taking possession of his imperial victim who is hearing the case of a poor peasant.

Death interrupts a courtly ceremonial and leads a well-born lady to the brink of an open grave to show to what lowness she must now descend.

Mediæval musicians: a miniature from a 14th-century manuscript of Boethius's *De Musica* (B.M. Burnley 275).

The York Cycle: the opening lines of a 15th-century manuscript of the Cutlers' play of the Conspiracy (B.M. Additional 35290).

contemporary woodcuts provide us with some idea of the mediæval imagination at work. The stained-glass in King's College Chapel, Cambridge, depicts several grotesque examples. The spectacle of black-faced devils pouring out of a painted hell-mouth, clad in scarlet cloaks, uttering harsh croaks and clashing pots and kettles, was likely to have provoked a mixed response of both laughter and fear, since one must remember that so far as the audience was concerned such ugly monsters did exist and lay in wait for the unwary. The denizens of Hell were solid, physically repulsive and acceptable on the stage only as comic figures, inevitably to be repelled and made to look absurd by the forces of righteousness.

Actors were paid. The performer who played God at Coventry received three and fourpence, the man who hanged Judas four-pence plus another fourpence for cock-crowing. Three and fourpence was half a mark, probably worth two or three guineas today, though equivalents are hard to determine. Chambers gives many details of the properties and the costumes; in the N-town cycle *Doomsday Play*, we are told that Hell's mouth required fire, a windlass and a barrel for the earthquake, and a Canterbury play on the Annunciation, no longer extant, required horses for the Magi made of hoops, laths and painted canvas. There are frequent references to actors riding horses in mediæval plays, not to mention oxen, asses and mares, and it was un-doubtedly easier to use real animals, at least when actual riding was demanded. Mak's 'child', however, would no doubt have been more suitably represented by a doll. The Norwich Grocers' play of Adam and Eve required a tail for the serpent, a face and hair for God the Father, hair for Adam and Eve and, most interesting of all, a 'rib coloured red'. Noah's Ark, however, was a more complicated property and to look convincing must have been a simple prefabricated device, with a sail, mast, helm, forecastle, door, window and three cabins set on a wheeled platform, to judge from Noah's soliloquy in the Wakefield pageant. Elaboration of stage properties was, as we have noted, one reason for the taking-over of performances by the trade guilds, who had the financial resources, but in the early days of the cycles the equipment was clearly of the simplest and even quaint, as Chambers's examples indicate.

The York cycle is the longest, most complete and best-known of the four extant cycles; it has been regularly performed in York since 1951 in a version lasting less than three hours. Canon J. B. Purvis of York Minster has rendered the Middle English into a modern English equivalent without sacrificing the metres, the extravagant alliterations and the earthy philological antiquity of the original. The so-called 'York metrist' developed the alliterative long line of Old English poetry, grouping his lines into eight-line stanzas *ababcddc* or occasionally *ababcccc*, and the opening play of the Creation, quoted on pages 18–20, is cast in lines divided by a medial pause with two stressed syllables in each 'hemistich' or half-line. The same author's *Resurrection* play is written in a six-line stanza rhyming *aaabab*, while his *Crucifixion* is done in a twelve-line stanza rhyming *abababababcdcd*. Purvis has succeeded in maintaining these complicated patterns to a remarkable extent and has also managed to preserve many idiomatic Yorkshire expressions current in the 14th century and still used in the 20th. Pilate dismisses Barabbas with the phrase 'Let him gang on his gate' (Let him go on his way), and the Middle English alliterative lines which mark the York playwright's fine touch are preserved with relatively little sacrifice of their subtlety. In the Cowpers' play of Man's disobedience and fall from Eden, Satan enters and addresses the audience:

Satanas: For woo my witte es in a were,
      That moffes me mykill in my mynde,
    The godhede þat I sawe so cleere,
      And parsayued þat he shuld take kynde,
            of a degree
    That he had wrought, and I denyed þat aungell kynde
              shuld it noȝt be;
     And we were faire and bright,
      Þerfore me thoght þat he

The kynde of vs tane myght,
And þer-at dedeyned me.

which becomes in Purvis's rendering:

For woe my wit works wildly here,
    Which moves me mickle in my mind,
The Godhead that I saw so clear,
    And perceived that he would take kind
                        Of a degree,
    That he had wrought,
    And I denied that angell kind
                Should it not be.

For we were fair and bright;
Therefore methought that he
Take one of us he might . . .
Yet he disdained me.

and in the Masons' and Goldsmiths' play, *The Coming of the Three Kings to Herod,* the resources of modern English are shown to be still astonishingly rich in alliterative range;

1 King: Hayle! þe fairest of felde folk for to fynde
        Fro the fende and his feeres faithefully vs fende,
        Hayll! þe best þat shall be borne to vnbynde
        All þe barnes þat are borne & in bale boune, . . .

becomes

Hail! Fairest of free folk to find,
From the fiend and his fellows in faith us defend
Hail, the best that shall be born to unbind
All the bairns that are born and in bale bound. . . .

The Lytsteres' (Dyers') play of Christ's trial before Herod opens with a raging speech by Herod:

Pes, ye brothellis and browlys, in þis broydenesse in brased,
And frekis þat are frendely your freykenesse to frayne,
Youre tounges fro tretyng of trifillis be trased,
Or þis brande þat is bright schall breste in youre brayne.
Plextis for no plasis, but platte you to þis playne,
And drawe to no drofyng, but dresse you to drede,
                        with dasshis.

which Purvis renders:

75

Peace, ye beggars and brats so broad and so bold,
Brave braggarts so bravely your boldness to boast;
From treating of trifles put reins on your tongues,
Or this brand that is bright shall burst in your brain.
Push not for places, but sit ye down plain;
Draw in no draffing, but dress you to dread;
                                        With dashes.

It is no easy task to uphold the alliterative vocabulary in modern English without falling into a near-nonsensical repetition of Middle English words, many of which have altered in meaning, and there is no doubt that an attempt such as Purvis's to reproduce Middle English poetic sounds in a modern context often suffers from its self-imposed discipline. Nevertheless, as an impression of the *sound* of Middle English rhetoric it is convincing in open-air performance, even though it may not always stand up to a close word-by-word analysis, for many of the lines are a cryptic mixture of two versions of English. Much the same was said by Ben Jonson about Spenser's experiment in *The Shepheardes Calender*, when he said of Spenser that 'he writ no language'; and Spenser's archaic-sounding English was really no farther away from that of Shakespeare than Purvis's rendering of the York plays is from its original. The translator's own explanation of his aims and method appears in the Foreword to his version. With the help of parallel passages, he shows how he had tried to surmount the difficulties of turning Northern Middle English into modern Yorkshire English, and points out, with examples, that the two dialects, so widely spaced in time, were not really so very different.

The cycle has now been performed for six seasons in the ruins of St. Mary's Abbey, as the principal event of the York Festival of the Arts. The high points are the Creation and Fall of the Angels, the Temptation, the expulsion of Adam and Eve from Eden, Noah's flood, the Cain and Abraham episodes, the Birth of Christ and the tyranny of Herod, the Passion, culminating in the Crucifixion and Resurrection and the Last Judgment. The chief characters include God, Christ, Gabriel, Lucifer or Satan, Adam and Eve, Noah and his wife, Cain and Abel, Abraham and Isaac, Herod, Pilate, Pharoah, John the Baptist, Annas, Caiaphas, Zaccheus, Mary the Mother, Joseph, Judas, Barabbas, Moses, the faithful disciples and the angels. There are also minor comic characters, such as Brewbarret, Cain's servant who makes a brief appearance when Cain is getting drunk after the murder of Abel, and various devils, the denizens of hell-mouth, who complain that Lucifer has brought about their expulsion from Heaven—three stanzas from their complaints are quoted on pages 19–20.

There are close to a hundred speaking parts in the cycle, and many crowd scenes, so that a great many people were given a chance to appear, possibly in some cases in traditionally-assigned parts. Roles such as those of God, Christ, Lucifer, Adam and Eve, Cain, Abraham and Isaac, Noah's wife and Herod were undoubtedly much coveted and made considerable demands on the skill of the actors. On the whole the freest acting is reserved for those who took parts involving some departure from the theological tradition, such as that of Noah's wife, which was played by a youth parodying the behaviour of a nagging spouse, though in the Chester cycle some women's parts were taken by women. Another in the same category was the part of Lucifer or Satan, which afforded considerable scope for an actor to project a 'devilish' personality, and in the temptation scenes to convey the insinuating argument of what Milton later called 'the spirited sly snake'. There are three Temptations in the cycle—that of Christ, that of Eve and that of Pilate's wife, called Percula in the play; she is made by Satan to dream that Christ is innocent so that he will not be condemned and his purpose to save Man's soul frustrated.

There are also many scattered small parts, of knights, soldiers, messengers, a beadle, councillors, maids and others, each capable of being given an individual interpretation and marking at an early period one of the striking features of English drama, particularly of comedy, which depends very much upon the flitting on and off the stage of minor figures, each making a fleeting but ineradicable impression on the audience before disappearing for ever. The Elizabethan play is full of them; any of

77

Shakespeare's plays yields its quota of supporting parts which, though short-lived and inessential so far as the main plot is concerned, challenge individual interpretative skill. Many of these parts could later be doubled, but in the trade guild cycles there was no need to do this. Since each trade guild put forward its own play, some of these small parts were created to satisfy individuals who wanted to act. Of course, the fact that most of the actors would have been personally known to the audience has to be considered when one is trying to imagine a 14th-century performance, and modern productions of the York cycle draw heavily on local schools and amateur drama groups, reserving only a few of the major roles for professionals imported from outside. In this way something of the intimacy of the cycles has been preserved.

THE GENESIS GROUP

The opening play of the Creation was given by the Barkers and has parts for from five to ten actors. It is made up of severely alliterative speeches, punctuated by the singing of the *Te Deum* and *Sanctus*. The main movement of the play comes in the actual fall of the angels (an episode based on apocryphal material and not on the Old Testament), and their howls and recriminations as they blame Lucifer for their loss of Heaven. Contrast is made between their bliss before the Fall and their succeeding woe. God makes two declamations, one at the beginning, establishing order so long as he is obeyed, and this is followed by a succession of utterances by angels. Lucifer's gradual assumption of power emerges in the words he speaks until, like Tamburlaine two centuries later, he is pronouncing himself God's peer. At this point he is hurled down and becomes Lucifer the Devil surrounded by other fallen angels, also metamorphosed into devils, jeering and yowling. The angel cherubim then announce the theological justification, and God ends the play with a second address informing the audience of his wrath, and resolving to create the world. This is an exposition of Old Testament Apocrypha, delivered from an elevated position, with God looking down at the audience as, with outstretched arms, he utters the metaphor of Creation.

And in my fyrste makyng to mustyr my mighte,
Sen erthe is vayne and voyde and myrknes emel,
I byd in my blyssyng ȝhe aungels gyf lyghte
To þe erthe, for it faded when the fendes fell.
In hell sall neuer myrknes be myssande,
Þe myrknes thus name I for nighte
The day þat call I this lyghte.

This play is succeeded by another, contributed by the Plasterers,
consisting entirely of a monologue by God, and a third, by the
Cardmakers, including God, Adam and Eve. In the fourth
play, performed by the Fullers, Adam and Eve are established
in Eden and are promising to obey God and not eat the apple
from the Tree of Knowledge.

The Temptation and Fall of Man is depicted in the Cowpers'
play which follows, composed of two dialogues. This is the
first play in the cycle to give the actors a strong opportunity
of interpreting the characters they are portraying, in this case
Adam, Eve and Satan, and to impose their own ideas of the
argument in mime while saying the words laid down for them
by the playwright. Listen to Satan tempting Eve:

Eva: Why what-kynne thyng art þou,
      Þat telles þis tale to me?
Sat.:   A worme þat wotith wele how
      Þat yhe may wirshipped be.
Eva: What wirshippe shulde we wynne ther-by?
      To ete þer-of us nedith it nought,
      We have lordshippe to make maistrie
        Of alle þynge þat in erthe is wrought.
Sat.:   Woman! do way!
      To gretter state ye may be broughte,
                and ye will do as I schall saye.
Eva: To do is vs full lothe,
      Þat shuld oure god myspaye.
Sat.:   Nay, certis it is no wathe,
      Ete it safely ye maye.
      For perille ryght þer none in lyes,
        But worshippe and a grete wynnynge,
      For ryght als god yhe shall be wyse,

And þere to hym in all-kyn thynge.
                        Ay! goddis shalle ye be!
Of ille and gode to haue knawyng,
                        For to be als wise as he.

Eva: Is þis soth þat þou sais?
Sat.: Yhe! why trowes þou noȝt me?
        I wolde be no-kynnes wayes
            Telle noȝt but trouthe to þe.
Eva: Than wille I to thy techyng traste,
        And fange þis frute unto owre foode.

                                    (*accepts the apple*)

Sat.: Byte on boldly, be nought a-basshed,
        And bere Adam to amende his mode,
                        And eke his blisse.

                                    (*Satan glides away*)

Eva: Adam! have here of frute full gode ...

The second dialogue, between Adam and Eve after he too has
eaten the apple, develops into a plausible conversation as the two
console each other before an angry God sends his Archangel to
drive them out of Paradise; in the following play of the
Armourers, Adam and Eve are given a spade and sent forth into
the world by the Archangel. They bicker and blame each other
for their plight and what they have to say is sometimes taken to
anticipate Milton's handling of the same situation in Book IX
of *Paradise Lost*, but Milton's quarrel-scene is far more complex
and subtle and there is not much more than a superficial resemblance in subject-matter. The dialogue in *Le Mystère d'Adam* is
superior.

This concludes the Genesis group. It is easily seen that the
plays are all short, unadorned, stay fairly close to the Vulgate
(the authorised Catholic Bible) and share the skeleton of the
plot among half a dozen guilds. Although they have about them
a didactic ring, this is not an obtrusion and there are some possibilities for experimenting with visual effects—the Fall of the
Angels, swinging on ropes and lowered unceremoniously from
the pageant-waggon to the ground, requires a two-tiered stage,
while God should be stationed at an even higher level, above
Paradise, to which Adam and Eve are conducted after their

Creation. When they also fall from grace, yet another lower level is required to represent Earth, making at least four levels of descent altogether. Aural effects include the singing of angel choirs before the Fall and the rumblings suggesting God's wrath after the Temptation. We have a record of some of the stage properties—it seems that Adam and Eve were dressed in leather skins, representing their nakedness. Although really a series of episodes, the action is continuous and imposes its own traditional unity, impressing the audience with a feeling of the historical inevitability of the events portrayed and providing an opportunity to share the remorse of Adam and Eve, as Scripture directs them to do, by involving themselves in the drama of an historical act which affects them all. However, compared with later plays, such as the Cain, the Abraham and the Passion, the Creation scenes in the York and other cycles are not much exploited dramatically, and even the personage of Satan emerges as little more than a conventional symbol. It was probably thought best by the promoters of the plays to leave the Genesis story in as untouched a condition as possible.

NOAH'S FLOOD

The next three plays depict the murder of Abel by Cain, the story of the building of the Ark and the entry of Noah, his wife and family, together with the animals, into the Ark, ending with their survival of the Flood. These three pieces were performed by the Glovers, Shipwrights, and Fishers and Mariners—the last two guilds rather appropriately. The Cain and Abel play is incomplete, and unfortunately the actual killing scene is among the parts lost, so that one may only imagine the opportunities for introducing stage violence. When the play resumes, a small comic part, that of Brewbarret or trouble-maker, is included and Cain gets drunk, providing comic relief before the angel enters to deliver the curse. The Wakefield Cain play is a much more exciting drama and will be discussed later. The Shipwrights' play is simply a duologue between God and Noah which paraphrases and expands the Vulgate account and does not permit much stage movement.

The Fishers' and Mariners' play is of a different order. In the 1966 production of the cycle, this play, an indispensable part of all the extant cycles, was taken out of the main series in St. Mary's Abbey and performed on a pageant-waggon which supported the Ark and a cast including God, the Noahs, their three sons and a whole host of imaginary animals. Yorkshire is a county with a fairly heavy rainfall, so it is not unlikely that flood effects were sometimes provided by nature. If not, the spectators were invited to picture in their mind's eye the rising of the flood waters as the rain fell incessantly for forty days and forty nights. The play is attractive to the critic chiefly because it includes Noah's wife, a nagger who complains of Noah's absence on the nights when he has been building the Ark. In the 1966 production, she boxes Noah's ears as he and his sons are dragging her, unwilling and protesting, on board the Ark, and there are many sparks of rough-and-ready humour which inject life into the dramatic sequences. Noah's wife is the ancestor of the many querulous shrews whom Elizabethan playwrights were so fond of portraying. The Flood pre-figures the Last Judgment, a symbolism which deters the playwright from allowing rough comedy to take over for any length of time. In the Newcastle play of the Flood, when Satan tempts Noah's wife with drink, encouraging her to give it to her husband, it is obvious that the playwright is pointing back at Eve's temptation.

The Wakefield Noah play is so critical of the wife that the bickering scenes have been interpreted as a reflection of the private life of the Wakefield Master. The wife has been complaining about Noah's absence and about the bare state of her cupboard. Noah answers that they are hard-pressed by new taxes, whereupon the wife says that he deserves to be beaten black and blue for his poor management, and addresses the wives in the audience, complaining of her burden and telling them how she is going to get her own back. Noah tells her crudely to shut up, whereupon they strike each other and there is an exchange of threats. Soon afterwards, however, Noah returns to his secret task, and when the Ark is ready and all are safely on board, including the uncooperative wife, there is another quarrel scene.

The wife wishes her husband were dead and is sure that women in the audience agree with her. Noah addresses himself to the men in the audience, saying:

Noe: Yee men that has wifis, whyls thay ar young,
        If ye luf youre lifis, chastice thare tong.
        Me thynk my hert ryfis, both levyr and long,
        To se sich stryfis, wedmen emong.
        Bot I,
        As haue I blys,
        Shall chastyse this.
Vxor: Yit may ye mys,
        Nicholl nedy!
Noe: I shall make þe still as stone, begynnar of blunder!
        I shall bete the bak and bone, and breke all in sonder.

and they fight until their sons intervene and the attention of the audience is once more centred on the plight of the Ark.

The possibilities for elaborate visual and aural effects are extensive and this is one miracle play which, as records show, required considerable expenditure in stage properties. The construction of the vessel was either mimed, with a large-scale model of the vessel already built, or put together from prefabricated pieces as Noah was speaking or, most likely of all, the Ark was wheeled in ready-made as he began his speech. In the Chester Flood play there are stage directions concerning the representation of the animals, as follows:

> Then noye shall goe into the arke with all his family, his wief except and the arke must be borded rounde about, and one the bordes all the beastes and fowles hereafter rehearsed must be painted that thes wordes may agree with the pictures . . .

while in another manuscript it is suggested that the pictures be on cards.

After this the family roll off the names of over fifty creatures, no doubt pointing in turn to each painted likeness. The Chester Ark is ready-made and the building is mimed by the family who 'shall make a signe as though they wrought vpon the shipe with diuers instrumentis'. The vessel is described in Genesis VI,

83

and depicted in several stained-glass windows; it took the form of a ship of the period, with embattled sides and three storeys. The birds which Noah sends out to test the level of the flood-waters, and which do not return, could have been live, but the dove bearing the olive-branch was to be 'let down from the mast by a cord', so was presumably a wooden substitute.

ABRAHAM AND ISAAC

Following the Noah play, and providing a strong contrast, is the *Sacrifice of Isaac*, played in the York cycle by the Parchemyners (parchment makers) and Bookbinders. This is an important play, although in fact the best dramatic version of the Abraham and Isaac story is not the York but the single Brome play, discovered last century at Brome Hall in Suffolk, which is dramatically more pungent. The plays continue the theme of obedience to God which runs through much of the cycle, and in fact the Chester *Sacrifice of Isaac* concludes with a heavy didactic statement of this underlying principle, referring by way of analogy to Christ's sacrifice.

The Abraham and Isaac play suggests a dilemma which fore-shadows the internal conflicts of Shakespeare's tragic heroes. Isaac was only a boy; in mediæval times a father's word was law and a child had to obey. This was the main dramatic impact on the contemporary audience. In addition, there is Man's theological duty to obey God, somewhat more abstract but equally immediate. The pattern of the drama soon asserts itself—Man must obey God and the Child must obey the Father—so that the dramatic conflict is one of duties. Abraham is ordered to sacrifice his son, whom he loves, by God whom he must obey. Isaac, ignorant of what fate awaits him, goes innocently with his father to perform the sacrifice and it is gradually revealed in conversation that Isaac, and not a beast of the field, is to be the victim. A snatch of their dialogue taken from the Chester play is given on page 12. Here is the equivalent passage from the Brome play, which is possibly a revision of the Chester version.

Isaac: Where is your quick beast that ye should kill?

84

Both fire and wood we have ready,
But quick beast have we none on this hill.

A quick beast, I wot well, must be dead
Your sacrifice for to make.

Abraham: Dread thee not, my child, I thee rede;
Our Lord will send me unto this stead
Some manner a beast for to take,
Through his sweet sand.

Isaac: Yea, father, but my heart beginneth to quake
To see that sharp sword in your hand.
Why bear ye your sword drawn so?
Of your countenance I have much wonder.

and, a few moments later, the poignancy of the occasion is intensified:

Abraham: Iwis, sweet son, I may not tell thee yet;
My heart is now so full of woe.

Isaac: Dear Father, I pray you, hide it not from me,
But some of your thought that ye tell me.

Abraham: Ah, Isaac, Isaac, I must kill thee!

Isaac: Kill me, father? Alas, what have I done?

If I have trespassed against you aught,
With a yard ye may make me full mild;
And with your sharp sword kill me nought,
For iwis, father, I am but a child.

Abraham: I am full sorry thy blood for to spill,
But truly, my child, I may not choose.

This is both the theological and the dramatic point of this austere play. Abraham has no choice and there is no conflict, for he is not, like Desdemona, torn between duty to father and duty to husband, nor, like Othello, turned into a tragic figure by his own actions in trying to resolve a conflict between his honour as a man and the claims of conjugal love. There is no tragedy, since Isaac is not sacrificed in the end, nor is there any doubt but that Abraham will obey God's will. In any case, deliberate sacrifice is not tragedy. Moreover, Isaac is a willing victim once he finds out that his sacrifice has been ordained by God, and only the interruption of the angel with a sheep for sacrifice instead of Isaac changes the course of action which scriptural authority had imposed on the characters. The play reflects a theological truth, not a human problem, and so it is wrong to describe it as a tragedy in modern terms or as exploring a conflict, since it does neither—nobody falls from grace, or loses his prosperity, nor is there any heroism in the accepted dramatic, that is, human sense of the word, though we can perhaps admire Abraham's rigid cleaving to duty. Isaac, though given some human reactions, is not a real 'boy' character, and in the York version makes little emotional impact, accepting his lot willingly.

Isaac: Why! fadir, will god þat I be slayne?
Abr.: ȝa, suthly, sone, so has he saide.
Isaac: And I sall noght grouche þer agayne,
     To wirke his wille I am wele payed;
     Sen it is his desire,
     I sall be bayne to be
     Brittynd and brent in fyre,
     And þer-fore morne noght for me.

The York cycle is theologically correct throughout, and has nothing like the human interest of certain of the related Wakefield plays, which blend grave and gay, grim and light-hearted, symbol and character in such a way as to show a clear dramatic advancement. For the historian the scriptural is linked with the secular play through the work of the anonymous Wakefield Master, the greatest humorist among the miracle playwrights.

OPPOSITION FROM THE CHURCH

Reference to the Wakefield Master's satiric compositions reminds us that the attitude to miracle plays, so far as official contemporary commentators were concerned, was hostile. A 14th-century Wycliffite sermon inveighing against miracle plays attacks them from a moral and religious point of view, and survives as representative of a species of prejudiced attacks on stage plays which started in the 2nd century and went on until the 17th. Miracles were suspect on moral grounds because, whatever their elevated claims as forms of worship, they were thought to breed false emotions due to mere play-acting and not to any revelation of sin. Miracles afford sensual delight and lead to wickedness, and the occasions on which they were played encouraged reckless spending and an indulgence in gluttony. The general thesis, with which the sermon opens, is that the representation of Christ's miracles on the stage was a desecration of sacred themes, and the anonymous author is as uncompromising as the early Church Fathers in his over-all condemnation.

However, it is apparent that while these extreme views may have been held by many Church dignitaries, they were not weighty enough to stop performances, though they may have acted as a corrective against elements thought to be sacrilegious. Miracle cycles were constantly under pressure from censorious individuals and bodies, and this pressure undoubtedly increased as the Reformation became more imminent. The official texts of the cycles which have come down to us are authorised and so it is a matter of speculation how closely live performers adhered to the lines set down for them; one is led by common sense to suspect a fairly continuous and healthy tension between players and ecclesiastical authorities.

The religious stage was one source of inspiration for the vivid pen and brush designs in late mediæval picture-bibles, which became a popular means of instruction during the 15th century, especially on the Continent. The drawings, vivid and spirited sketches, include a variety of scenes, almost certainly taken from acted episodes. Expressions of anger, malice, treachery, amiability and round-eyed piety suggest that stark realism was the artist's main object. Inter-relations between the plays and contemporary religious art have lately become the focus of scholarly investigation in the light of these picture-bibles, for these illustrated devotional narratives were part of the contemplative world of mediæval people and reflect the same intensity of feeling that characterises their drama. The picture titles often occur in stage directions given in manuscripts of miracle plays, indicating a strong connection with the religious drama. (See opposite page 73.)

5

Realism in the Miracle Plays

14th-century vernacular religious drama is the result of the coming together of several trends; the liturgical trend, which was solemn and serious, the didactic trend, which was directed to teaching the facts of the Bible to unlettered people, and the popular trend, which was a mixture of satire, usually political, aimed at contemporaries, and naïve comedy of the knock-about kind, with plenty of boisterous action. These early playwrights wanted to improve the appeal of their plays by including both verbal and visual attractions, and their scenes mingle quick-witted repartee with slapstick vulgarity. Take, for example, the Wakefield play of Cain and Abel, performed by the Glovers' guild.

Abell: God, as he both may and can,
   Spede the, brother, & thi man.
Cayn: Com kis myne ars! Me list not ban;
   As welcom standys theroute.
   Thou shuld haue bide til thou were cald;
   Com nar, and other drife or hald——
   And kys the dwillis toute!
   Go grese this shepe vnder the toute,
   For that is the moste lefe.

and later:

Abell: Brother, as elders haue vs kend,
   First shuld we tend with oure hend,
   And to his lofyng sithen be brend.
Cayn: My farthyng is in the preest hand
   Syn last tyme I offyrd.

Cain then tries to dodge payment of his tithe by deliberately miscounting the sheaves he is supposed to offer to God, and when he is cautioned by Abel, rudely replies:

Cayn: Yei, kys the dwills ars behynde!
 The dwill hang the bi the nek!
 How that I teynd, neuer thou rek.
 Will thou not yit hold thi peasse?
 Of this ianglyng I reyde thou seasse,
 And teynd I well, or, tend I ill,
 Bere the euen & speke bot skill.
 Bot now, syn thou has teyndid thyne,
 Now will I set fyr on myne.   (*Tries to burn his tithe*)

He does so, and is almost choked by a billow of black smoke.

Cayn: We! out! haro! help to blaw!
 It will not bren for me, I traw;
 Puf! this smoke dos me mych shame—   (*Blows on it*)
 Now bren in the dwillys name!
 A! what dwill of hell is it?
 Almost had myne breth beyn dit;
 Had I blawen oone blast more,
 I had beyn choked right thore.
 It stank like the dwill in hell,
 That longer ther myght I not dwell.
Abell: Cam, this is not worth oone leke;
 Thy tend shuld bren withoutten smeke.
Cayn: Com kys the dwill right in the ars!
 For the it brens bot the wars.
 I wold that it were in thi throte,
 Fyr, and shefe, and ich a sprote.

At this point in the proceedings, God appears and looks reprovingly down on Cain.

Deus: Cam, whi art thou so rebell
 Agans thi brother Abell?
 Thar thou nowther flyte ne chyde.
 If thou tend right thou gettys thi mede;
 And be thou sekir, if thou teynd fals,
 Thou bese alowed ther after als.

This does not make any impression on Cain, who sneers:

Cayn: Whi, who is that hob-ouer-the-wall?
        We! who was that that piped so small?
        Com, go we hens, for perels all;
        God is out of hys wit!

The First Murderer is here depicted as a familiar type of mediæval ploughman, neglectful of his work, rough-spoken and contemptuous of authority, distrustful of the motives of others and unrepentant to the last. God is not so much a mystical personage as a type of the 14th-century tax-gatherer, and Cain addresses him as such. The fourth character, Garcio, a boy, is a foil to Cain and treats him with sly insolence, mocking his own hungry condition as a serf as he echoes Cain's proclamation with witty asides.

Cayn: I commaund you in the kyngys nayme,
Garcio: And in my masteres, fals Cayme,
Cayn: That no man at thame fynd fawt ne blame,
Garcio: Yey, cold rost is at my masteres hame.
Cayn: Nowther with hym nor with his knafe,
Garcio: What! I hope my master rafe.
Cayn: For thay ar trew full many fold.
Garcio: My master suppys no coyle bot cold.
Cayn: The kyng wrytys you vntill.
Garcio: Yit ete I neuer half my fill.
Cayn: The kyng will that thay be safe.
Garcio: Yey, a draght of drynke fayne wold I hayfe.
Cayn: At thare awne will let tham wafe.
Garcio: My stomak is redy to recyfe.
Cayn: Loke no man say to theym, on nor other—
Garcio: This same is he that slo his brother.
Cayn: Byd euery man thaym luf and lowt.
Garcio: Yey, ill-spon weft ay comes foule out.
Cayn: Long or thou get thi hoyse, and thou go thus aboute.
         Byd euery man theym pleasse to pay.
Garcio: Yey, gif Don, thyne hors, an wisp of hay.

The satire completely outweighs the theology, and the personality of Cain may well be modelled on that of some local worthy, whose habits of speech were known to the Wakefield citizenry. Caricatures drawn 'to the life' are apparent in many plays in the Wakefield cycle.

THE CRUCIFIXION

A different kind of incongruity is evident in the York play of the Crucifixion as performed by the 'Pynners, Latoners and Payntours'. The conversation of the soldiers nailing Christ to the cross has a rough humour about it and it is likely that the actor playing the part of Christ uttered loud yells as the soldiers went through the motions of hammering in the nails. Such a scene emphasised that the object of the performance was to recreate a historical event imaginatively rather than in the abstract, for although some of these episodes may be out of place in a biblical context, they are certainly not so in a realistic context, and several modern reconstructions of miracle plays show a common-sense concern with this fidelity of representation. Here is a section taken from the dialogue of the men nailing Jesus to the cross.

i Mil.:	Why carpe ʒe so? faste on a corde,
	And tugge hym to, by toppe and taile.
iii Mil.:	ʒa, þou comaundis lightly as a lorde,
	Com helpe to haale, with ille haile.
i Mil.:	Nowe certis þat schall I doo,
	Full suerly as a snayle.
iii Mil.:	And I schall tacche hym too,
	Full nemely with a nayle.
	Þis werke will holde, þat dar I heete,
	For nowe are feste faste both his handis.
iv Mil.:	Go we all foure þanne to his feete,
	So schall oure space be spedely spende.
ii Mil.:	Latte see, what bourde his bale myght beete,
	Tharto my bakke nowe wolde I bende.
iv Mil.:	Owe! þis werke is all vnmeete,
	This boring muste all be amende.
i Mil.:	A! pees man, for mahounde,
	Latte noman wotte þat wondir,

A roope schall rugge hym doune,
Yf all his synnous go a-soundre.

ii Mil.: Þat corde full kyndely can I knytte,
Þe comforte of þis karle to kele.
i Mil.: Feste on þanne faste þat all be fytte,
It is no force howe felle he feele.
ii Mil.: Lugge on ȝe both a litill ȝitt.
iii Mil.: I schalle noughte sese, as I haue seele.
iv Mil.: And I schall fonde hym for to hitte.
ii Mil.: Owe, haylle!
iv Mil.: Hoo nowe, I halde it wele.
i Mil.: Haue done, dryue in þat nayle,
So þat no faute be foune.
iv Mil.: Þis wirkyng wolde noȝt faile,
Yf foure bullis here were boune.

Later on, the four of them try to raise the cross, with its
burden, to a vertical position, and the dialogue becomes sharply
ironic as they complain about the pain in back and shoulder
and the physical difficulty which their task involves. Finally
they set the cross up, and ask the crucified victim, with exaggerated politeness:

i Mil.: Say, sir, howe likis þou nowe,
Þis werke þat we haue wrought?
iv Mil.: We praye youe sais vs howe.
ȝe fele, for faynte ȝe ought?

Jesus then answers:

Jesus: Al men þat walkis by waye or strete,
Takes tente ȝe schalle no trauayle tyne,
By-holdes myn heede, myn handis, and my feete,
And fully feele nowe or ȝe fyne,
Yf any mournyng may be meete
Or myscheue mesured vnto myne
My Fadir, þat alle bales may bete,
For-giffis þes men þat dois me pyne.
What þai wirke wotte þai noght,
Therfore my Fadir I craue

> Latte neuere þer synnys be sought,
> But see þer saules to saue.

whereupon the soldiers jeer at the spectacle:

i Mil.: We! harke! he jangelis like a jay.
ii Mil.: Me thynke he patris like a py.
iii Mil.: He has ben doand all þis day,
And made grete meuyng of mercy.

The play appeals directly to the audience without overmuch subtlety and the unknown author is clearly adept at presenting the physically horrible. The scene is long-drawn-out and the part quoted above, wherein Christ's body is stretched with cords in order to bring his limbs as far as the nail-holes is, as one may understand from the dialogue, made even more grotesque by the lumpish jests of the clumsy workmen. The properties, hammers, nails, cords, cross and blood, probably pig's blood, could be used to great effect by competent actors.

All the miracle play cycles concentrate on the Crucifixion drama, though the York and Wakefield versions are far less restrained than the Chester and N-town ones, both of which limit the roles of the soldiers. The liturgical drama avoided laying stress on the Passion, perhaps because this part of the playwright's subject had been fulfilled by the Mass, but as the drama moved farther away from the liturgy, the various stages of the Passion were given a greater prominence. The plays of the Buffeting and the Scourging, which precede the Crucifixion, gave actors a good deal of scope for horseplay and pandered to popular delight in knock-about action.

We must remember that a 14th-century audience knew the Crucifixion scene to be the justification both of the scenes preceding it and of the others concluding the cycle, for it was a re-enactment of the Truth on which their faith depended. This is not so in the case of a modern spectator, who is more likely to be drawn purely and simply by the horrible fascination of a public execution, or, on the other hand, repelled by such stark realism. In the 1951 production of the York cycle, the church authorities persuaded the producer to modify this scene on the

93

grounds that it was too cruel, but more recent productions, particularly that of 1963, have not been constrained to pander to the finer feelings of a fastidious modern audience. At the time when the York cycle was being composed, executions served both as a warning and an entertainment. From the 11th century, English towns began to acquire charters granting them rights of self-government, and most of these permitted rough-and-ready methods of dealing with lawbreakers, particularly those found guilty of crimes concerning personal property. Hanging, flogging, maiming and branding, often for offences which we should consider minor, were standard punishments. The citizens of York would be expected to enjoy an execution scene and to learn from it, even when it was only a simulated one depicting a method of capital punishment not practised in England. Their interest was rooted in the fact that they were seeing a particular execution of a historical person, not weakly symbolised or suggested but repeated in every detail. The reality of it made the Resurrection all the more wonderful. In the York cycle, the play was performed, doubtless with some implied irony, by the Butchers; it shows that the author had a considerable mastery of natural dialogue reflecting the sort of crude colloquial talk which one might expect from the lips of common executioners and torturers, who were a despised breed, fit only to be shunned and abused by law-abiding folk.

THE HOMILETIC TRADITION

The raw details of the Passion itself would have been well known to the spectators, since pulpit rhetoricians from St. Bernard onwards had established a strong tradition of lurid description of how the actual crucifixion was carried out. We have a number of these highly-coloured accounts, and it is clear from reading them where the playwrights found their inspiration for scenes of flagellation and physical torture. Here is an extract from one such homily, turned into modern English:

> He was beaten and buffeted, scorned and scourged, until he had hardly a whole piece of skin left from head to foot big enough for a man to put the point of a needle. All over his body a stream

94

of blood ran freely. He was crowned with a garland of thorns as a mark of derision. And when the crown, according to writers, would not stay firmly and fast on his head because of the long strong thorns, they took sticks to beat it down till the thorns pierced the brain pan. He was nailed hand and foot with sharp rough nails so that his agony should be the greater and so finally he suffered the most painful death, hanging with great shame on the cross.

From the same sources details of the interior of Hell were easily obtained. A sermon preached in London in 1406 described the fate of the cursed in these graphic terms:

> And there they shall be boiled in fire and brimstone without end. Venomous worms and adders shall gnaw all their members without ceasing and the worm of conscience which complains inwardly shall gnaw the soul . . . now you may weep and howl! Now your lot is everlasting bitterness; your frolic is turned to mourning, your laughing to sorrow and your tears shall be comfortless and eternal. The fire that torments you shall never be quenched and they who torture you shall never become weary and shall never die.

The most popular of the homiletic works drawn upon by the preachers was the *Pricke of Conscience*, which is strong in terrifying physical descriptions of Hell as an infernal oven, where the shrieking of the tortured mingle with the yells of devils tormenting them, so that in their uncontrollable frenzy they tear one another to pieces. A contrasting picture is given by another homilist of the bliss which awaits those who go to Paradise:

> Thy body shall then be glorified. That body which is now so heavy and so clumsy will be as bright as the sun . . . then when there will have been more bodies gathered together than there are stars in the heavens or gravel in the sea and every single one of them is so very bright, then there will be a glorious sight, but even that shall be like a shadow when compared with the brightness of the blessed face of God.

There are no scenes of the interior of Hell or of Paradise in any of the miracle plays, but there was an artificial hell-mouth, and the homilists had made sure that no one was in much doubt as to where, symbolically, it led. The concluding play in the cycles, that of the Last Judgment, depended very much for its moral effect on an imaginary Hell, to which the criminals and rogues of this world were to be consigned by Christ, the Chief Justice. In the Wakefield Judgment play, the first half depicts the now repentant inhabitants of Hell when the Last Trump is sounded. There are four Evil Souls, two Demons, a demonic personage called Tutivillus, Four Good Souls, an Angel, and Jesus in this play, which takes place on earth, in Hell and in Heaven. The hand of the Wakefield Master is obvious and this particular Judgment drama is, though similar to the York pageant on the same subject, very much more lively. The influence of the preacher is evident in every line, for the play is a transmutation of the homilist's narrative in the *Pricke of Conscience* and other monitory works:

Secundus Malus: Alas, I stande great aghe / to loke on that Iustyce,
Ther may no man of lagh / help with no quantyce.
vokettys ten or twelfe / may none help at this nede,
Bot ilk man for his self / shall answere for his dede.

Quartus Malus: Wo worth euer the fader / that gate me to be borne!
That euer he lete me stir / bot that I had bene forlorne;
Warid be my moder / and warid be the morne
That I was borne of hir / alas, for shame and skorne!

The Demons of Hell inform us of the kind of people who are about to be damned:

Secundus Demon: Of Wraggers and wrears / a bag full of brefes,
Of carpars and cryars / of mychers and thefes,
Of lurdans and lyars / that no man lefys,
Of flytars, of flyars / and renderars of reffys;

Primus Demon: has thou oght Writen there / of the femynyn gendere?

Secundus Demon: yei, mo then I may bere / of rolles forto render;
Thai ar euer as a spere / if thai seme bot slender;
Thai ar euer in were / if thai be tender, yll fetyld;

Later, when Tutivillus joins them, the subject of women is again taken up, their 'powder and paint' and, ironically, in the words of Tutivillus:

Tutiuillus: She lookys like a saynt,
       And wars then the deyle.

This castigation of the female sex was a commonplace of mediæval preachers, who followed the tradition of St. Jerome in their condemnation of the daughters of Eve as snares for men, in odd contrast to their veneration for Mary, the perfect example of womankind.

One vivid picture succeeds another as various classes are pilloried by the merciless satirist. An overdressed servant, strutting like a lord:

> his luddokkys thai lowke / like walk-mylne cloggys,
> his hede is like a stowke / hurlyd as hoggys,
> A woll blawen bowke / thise friggys as froggys . . .

and a gaily-attired maid whose garment

> . . . is open behynde,
> before is it pynde,
> Bewar of the West wynde
>   youre smok lest it wafe.

These ludicrous figures represent Pride, which is followed by more of the Seven Deadly Sins, Anger, Envy, Covetousness and Gluttony, all familiar figures, drunkards, belching and vomiting, quarrelling all night long with their tipsy companions. Not far behind is Sloth and a whole host of 'howndys of hell':

> And ye Ianetyys of the stewys / and lychoures on lofte,
> youre baill now brewys / avowtrees full ofte,
> youre gam now grewys / I shall you set softe,
> youre sorow enewes / com to my crofte
>   All ye;
> All harlottys and horres,
> And bawdys that procures,
> To bryng thaym to lures
>   Welcom to my see!

> Ye lurdans and lyars / mychers and thefes,
> fflytars and flyars / that all men reprefes,
> Spolars, extorcyonars / Welcom, my lefes!
> ffals Iurars and vsurars / to symony that clevys,
>   To tell;

> hasardars and dysars,
> ffals dedys forgars,
> Slanderars, bakbytars,
>   All vnto hell.

This queue of entrants to Hell has made the porter at the gates work especially hard; the increase of the wicked makes the first demon think that Judgment Day is not far off, and the two demons, carrying their lists, make their way to the Judgment Hall. The derisive laughter of the audience as the villains are displayed and transfixed is suddenly quieted. As Jesus appears, the mood of the drama abruptly changes from hilarity to high seriousness.

Jesus makes a speech, announcing his purpose now that 'this wicked world is spent' and recapitulates his Passion, showing his wounds, exposing the deeds of the guilty and the innocent. The Good Souls he sends to Heaven, the Evil Souls to Hell, and the Demons and Tutivillus come forward to bear witness against the objects of their satirical attacks, whom they carry off kicking and screaming.

Primus Demon: sir, I trow thai be dom / somtyme were full melland;
                Will ye se how thai glom. / thou art ay telland.
Secundus Demon: Now shall thai haue rom / in pyk and tar euer dwelland,
                Of thare sorow no some / bot ay to be yelland
                  In oure fostre.

and at the end, one of the Good Souls informs the audience:

Primus Bonus: We loue the, lorde, in alkyn thyng,
                That for thyne awne has ordand thus,
           That we may haue now oure dwellyng
                In heuen blis giffen vnto vs.
           Therfor full boldly may we syng
                On oure way as we trus;
           Make we all myrth and louyng
                With te deum laudamus.

Scenes like these make it quite clear that the miracle cycles should not simply be regarded as independent manifestations of the ability of a group of individual playwrights to devise dramatic sequences in the vernacular but as having close links with popular homiletic material and with a long tradition of popular preaching. They are not tedious moralising discourses, but vital colourful narratives of man in his society, exhortations to repentance and terrifying glimpses of a physical hell beyond the experience of any contemporary hearers but not, let it be said, unknown to our age of Nazi concentration camps and Hitler-inspired atrocities. In fact, no mediæval homilist ever imagined a hell to equal the man-made savageries of Belsen or Auschwitz, Ravensbrück or Dachau.

THE 'SECOND SHEPHERDS' PLAY'

One play in the Wakefield cycle stands in a class by itself. This is the *Secunda Pastorum* or *Second Shepherds' Play*. All the cycles include Shepherds' Plays, which take their origin from liturgical *pastores*, in their turn developed from a Christmas trope (see page 29). This is why they have so much in common. They all require two scenes, the first in the fields where the shepherds are tending their flocks and are informed of the Nativity by the Angel, the second in the stable where the Child lies in a crib watched over by the Holy figures. Between the two scenes there is an interval in both space and time, representing the journey made by the Shepherds, or sometimes by the Magi. Except for the N-town *Shepherds' Play*, which stays close to Bible-history, all these *pastores* include secular action. Both the Chester and the Wakefield plays mirror contemporary life. The *Secunda Pastorum* is unique because it contains a comic double-plot.

The three shepherds are English, with rustic names, Col, Gib and Daw, and they make homespun complaints. The first shepherd grumbles about the weather, cruel taxation of the poor and the cocky feudal retainers who help to grind down the labouring class. The second shepherd repeats some of this but his main trouble is a marital one and he issues a warning against marriage before describing his wife in graphic terms:

Secundus pastor: ffor, as euer red I pystyll / I haue oone to my fere,
As sharp as a thystyll / as rugh as a brere;

99

She is browyd lyke a brystyll / with a sowre loten chere;
had She oones Wett Hyr Whystyll / She couth Syng full
clere

    Hyr pater noster.
She is as greatt as a whall,
She has a galon of gall:
By hym that dyed for vs all,
    I wald I had ryn to I had lost hir.

The third shepherd compares the rainstorm to Noah's flood,
bewailing the poor treatment and lack of nourishment which
is his own miserable lot:

Tercius pastor: for the fayr that ye mak,
    I shall do therafter / wyrk as I take;
    I shall do a lytyll, sir / and emang euer lake,
    ffor yit lay my soper / neuer on my stomake
      In feyldys.

After some more talk in the same vein and a song for three
voices, the trio are joined by Mak, a sheep-stealer and a parody
on the Angel visitant. Mak at first pretends to be a nobleman's
henchman, imitating southern English speech, and demanding
respect, but the shepherds know him and his reputation. However, they let him lie down and sleep between them after
listening to his own complaints about hunger, greedy wife and
fast-growing family:

Mak: Bot were I not more gracyus / and rychere befar,
    I were eten outt of howse / and of harbar;
    Yit is she a fowll dowse / if ye com nar:
    Ther is none that trowse / nor knowys a war,
      Then ken I.
    Now wyll ye se what I profer,
    To gyf all in my cofer
    To morne at next to offer
      hyr hed mas penny.

They lie down to sleep, Mak utters a snatch of fake Latin and
when he is sure that they are unconscious he rises and casts a

pagan spell on them so that he may 'borrow' a sheep without being interrupted. He takes one and goes home with it.

The next scene shows us Mak's cottage, and his wife, Gil, who is annoyed at being interrupted in her spinning. He produces the sheep, they squabble and she warns him that one day he will be caught and hanged. Mak wants to kill the sheep and dine well for the first time in over a year, but Gil is afraid that the shepherds may hear the animal bleating as it is slaughtered and suggests that it be put into a cradle and passed off as their newly-born son—an idea for which Mak's previous conversation with the shepherds has prepared both them and the audience. The presence of a new-born baby could thus be easily accounted for. Mak then returns to the shepherds, who are still sleeping, and have not noticed his absence.

The following episode begins with the shepherds waking up uttering some bad Latin and going their separate ways, but agreeing to meet later after they have made certain that their sheep are unharmed. Mak excuses himself, saying that he had dreamed his wife had given birth to 'a young lad'. We are now taken to Mak's cottage, where he and Gil are getting ready to throw the shepherds off the scent. Gil swaddles the sheep in the cradle and tells Mak to sing a lullaby while she herself groans as if in pain. When the shepherds arrive, the first having discovered his loss and the other two highly suspicious of Mak or Gil, or both, the real comic section of the play gets under way. Mak tells lies, twists and turns, alternates feigned innocence with bluster and begs pity for his wife in her agony. The shepherds eventually swallow Mak's story and take themselves off, but return a few moments later bringing sixpence as a gift for the 'baby'. After some further exchanges, they recognise the sheep in a hilarious sequence:

3 Pastor: Gyf me lefe hym to kys, and lyft vp the clowtt.

(*Takes a peep*)

What the dewill is this? He has a long snowte!
1 Pastor: He is merkyd amys. We wate ill abowte.
2 Pastor: Ill-spon weft, Iwys, ay commys foull owte.

(*Recognises the sheep*)

Ay, so!
He is lyke to oure shepe!

3 *Pastor:* How, Gyb, may I pepe?

1 *Pastor:* I trow kynde will crepe
Where it may not go.

2 *Pastor:* This was a qwantt gawde and a far-cast:
It was a hee frawde.

3 *Pastor:*   Yee, syrs, wast.
Lett bren this bawde and bynd hir fast.
A fals skawde hang at the last;
So shall thou.
Wyll ye se how thay swedyll
His foure feytt in the medyll?
Sagh I neuer in a credyll
A hornyd lad or now.

Mak: Peasse, byd I. What, lett be youre fare.
I am he that hym gatt, and yond woman hym bare.

1 *Pastor:* What dewill shall he hatt, Mak? Lo, God makys ayre!
Lett be all that! Now God gyf hym care,
I sagh.

Vxor: A pratty child is he
As syttys on a wamans kne;
A dyllydowne, perdé,
To gar a man laghe.

Eventually Mak is forced to ask for mercy and the three shepherds toss him in a canvas blanket by way of punishment.

This concludes the pseudo-nativity and the remaining episodes make up the genuine nativity. The shepherds fall asleep and an Angel sings *Gloria in Excelsis* and enjoins them to seek the child at Bethlehem. In the final scene the shepherds hail the Infant Christ and present their symbolic gifts, a bunch of cherries, a bird and a ball. They learn of the child's identity from Mary and the play concludes with a song by the shepherds as they depart rejoicing. There are several local references, many colloquial idioms are put into the mouths of the characters, especially Mak, and the piece has about it a delightful freshness and a simple profundity which a live performance brings out.

The *First Shepherds' Play* is more obviously serious but is also embellished with social satire and relieved by comic dialogue and ribald tomfoolery. The influence of a pre-Christian folklore is strong, and the familiar complaints about poverty and harsh landlords are banished by the shepherds' mock-banquet, made up of a strange assortment of invisible aristocratic and peasant fare; the irony is savage:

primus pastor:	here a foote of a cowe / well sawsed, I wene,
	The pestell of a sowe / that powderd has bene,
	Two blodyngis, I trow / A leueryng betwene; . . .
ijus pastor:	I haue here in my mayll / sothen and rost,
	Euen of an ox tayll / that wold not be lost;
	ha, had goderhayll! / I let for no cost,
	A good py or we fayll, / this is good for the frost
	In a mornyng;
	And two swyne gronys,
	All a hare bot the lonys,
	we myster no sponys
	here, at oure mangyng.
iijus pastor:	here is to recorde / the leg of a goys,
	with chekyns endorde / pork, partryk, to roys;
	a tart for a lorde / how thynk ye this doys?
	a calf lyuer skorde / with the veryose;
	Good sawse,
	This is a restorete
	To make a good appete.

But the nativity scene, ushered in by a heavenly choir singing *Gloria in Excelsis*, has a grave delicacy; in this and in the Chester play of the Shepherds, the satirical elements and topical allusions loom large, almost distorting the joyful message of nativity. Several modern critics have concluded that these comic elements sometimes break the mood and work against the playwright's intention. There is something to be said for this view if the antics of the thief and the buffoonery of the shepherds do in fact draw an individual reader away from the main thread of the play, but to judge one of these plays out of its cyclic and historical context is to impose a post-Reformation standard of the study on what was essentially a mediæval show having its own special qualities. Sacred drama was not profaned by the inclusion of secular or even pagan elements. The *Secunda Pastorum* appealed to a peasant audience partly because it emphasised the concerns of the English labourer side by side with the miracle of the Nativity. By placing one in juxtaposition with the other the Wakefield Master bridged the gap in space and time between England, Bethlehem and the world eternal. The purgative effect of un-restrained laughter linked animal to spiritual and Man to God just as the various parodies of church services around Christmas and New Year, the Feast of Fools, the vesting of the Boy Bishop or of the Lord of Misrule, were intended to do.

The Feast of Fools flourished in France and England during the 12th and 13th centuries and continued until the mid-17th century. In this ceremony, an ass was led into the church, the celebrant brayed a mock Mass while the clerics, dressed as women, danced in the choir. Black puddings were eaten and dice games played on the altar, while a pair of old shoes were burned in the censers. Thus were the grotesque and the pious intermingled. From this pagan licence came the comic spirit of the mediæval play, and although it is certainly not easy for us to comprehend, the Wakefield audience would not have found that the double-plot of the *Secunda Pastorum* violated any theological tradition. When the angel appears, the yokels find that they have been singled out for the especial purpose of greeting the Christ-child. In a mediæval sermon, an amusing parable might be interjected into a serious exposition of the Nativity: the same thing happens in such plays as the *Secunda Pastorum*. The Mak episode is borrowed from a common European folk-tale just like the story of the Colbek dancers, put to similar use by the author of *Handlyng Synne*.

METRICAL INGENUITY

It will have been noticed that the plays of the Wakefield Master are metrically ingenious. His characteristic stanza is a nine-lined one, rhyming *aaaabcccb*, with internal rhymes in the first four lines or quatrain. A more detailed account of the stanzaic complications in the plays may be found in Professor A. C. Cawley's *The Wakefield Pageants in the Towneley Cycle* (Appendix II). This stanza with its derivatives is unique in mediæval literature; the Master either invented it himself or remodelled it from some unidentified source. Whatever its origins, it is flexible, useful for quick speech, monologue or dialogue, can register changes in mood and, because of its internal variations, may be clearly distributed between as many as four speakers, as for example in:

2 Pastor: Mak, freyndys will we be, for we are all oone.
Mak:　　We? Now I hald for me, for mendys gett I none.
　　　　　Fare well all thre! All glad were ye gone.
3 Pastor: Fare wordys may ther be, bot lufe is ther none
　　　　　this yere.
1 Pastor: Gaf ye the chyld any thyng?
2 Pastor: I trow not oone farthyng.
3 Pastor: Fast agane will I flyng;
　　　　　Abyde ye me there.

Sometimes two speakers may share a single line:

1 Pastor: Now, as euer haue I blys, to the bothom it is sonken
2 Pastor: Yit a botell here is—
3 Pastor:　　　　　That is well spoken
　　　　　By my thrift we must kys!
2 Pastor:　　　　　—that had I forgoten.

Generally, the Master exhibits a high degree of versatility in inventing rhymes, alliterative phrases, sound effects and plays on word-endings; this suggests an experimental enthusiasm well in advance of its time, anticipating the delight in verbal display of Skelton and the early Tudors.

TYRANTS—HEROD AND PILATE

Another play which reflects contemporary life directly is the Wakefield Master's play *Herod the Great*. Herod, Pilate and Pharaoh all stand as types of the feudal tyrant. The tradition of

Herod as a rumbustious angry man goes back to Matthew II, 16 and Hamlet reminds us in his speech to the players that overdone wrath 'out-Herods Herod' and is to be avoided by good actors. The figure of Herod also looks forward to Macbeth, who is driven by fear and ambition to deeds of violence and greed. The Herod of the Wakefield play introduces himself as a bombastic conqueror, a prototype of Tamburlaine, dressed like a mediæval ruler, and calling for silence as he enters—this indicates that the audience was expected to hiss and jeer at him as a known 'villain'. His speeches are of the ranting sort and his bullying is that of a social climber who seeks homage from the barons whose backing he is ready to buy in the most blatant fashion. He suffers, in addition, from the paranoid delusion that the three Kings of the Epiphany, in alliance with the child Christ, are conspiring against him. To make sure that he himself will survive, he will stop at nothing and his lurid speech makes him more than the stock angry man, for he is greedy and possessed by a blood-lust which he ruthlessly indulges.

Herod: welcom, lordyngys, Iwys / both greatt and small!
The cause now is this / that I send for you all:
A lad, a knafe, borne is / that shuld be kyng ryall;
Bot I kyll hym and his / I wote I brast my gall;
   Therfor, Syrs,
Veniance shall ye take,
All for that lad sake,
And men I shall you make
   where ye com ay where, syrs.

To bedlem loke ye go / And all the coste aboute,
All knaue chyldren ye slo / and lordys, ye shalbe stoute;
Of yeres if they be two / and within, of all that rowte
On lyfe lyefe none of tho / that lygys in swedyll clowte,
   I red you;
Spare no kyns bloode,
let all ryn on floode,
If women wax woode;
   I warn you, syrs, to spede you;

The York play of Herod is weaker in its representation of the chief character; though the opening speech, quoted on page 75, is poetically exciting, the rest of the dialogue is unremarkable, and there is little action.

In the Chester cycle Herod's son is among those put to death by his own order, and his nurse rages at Herod himself, whereupon Herod is forced to admit that

Herode: He was right sicker in silk aray,
        in gould, and pyrrye that was so gay,
        they might well know by his aray,
        he was a kinges sonne.

In this version, Herod the monster dies and is dragged off by a lusty Demon:

Demon: Ther fire burnes bloe and brent
        he shall be ther, this lord, verament,
        his place euermore therin is hent,
        his body neuer to goe froe;

Thus justice is seen to be done and, as the body of Herod is dragged off by the fiend, a complete contrast of mood is established by the reappearance of an angel who had previously warned Joseph and Mary to take the Christ-child to Egypt, and now returns to command them to return to Judaea. The play ends with a song by the angel, bringing peace where a short time before violence had reigned.

Another distinctive character is Pilate, who appears in all the cycles. As the judge who condemns Christ, he is a prominent figure in five plays in the Wakefield cycle, six in the York, and comes into the two longer Chester plays as well as the N-town cycle and the Cornish trilogy. Pilate is both hero and villain—he tried to save Christ and he condemned him—so that his characterisation is usually more indistinct than that of most miracle play personages. The Wakefield Pilate is strongly depicted as a villain, a dramatic contrast to Jesus. The York Pilate is anxious to save Jesus and is generally humane. The Chester and N-town Pilates are vacillating and do not emerge as prominent personalities. On the whole, mediæval portraits of Pilate are in the tradition of the canonical Gospels and show

him in a sympathetic light. Even when he rants and raves, as in
the York play, his bark is worse than his bite, for he is always
advising against intemperate action. Only in the Wakefield play
is Pilate cast consistently as an unjust judge. In *The Conspiracy*,
he starts off by informing the audience of the kind of power he
holds.

Pilatus: ffor I am he that may / make or mar a man;
       My self if I it say / as men of cowrte now can;
       Supporte a man to day / to-morn agans hym than,
       On both parties thus I play / And fenys me to ordan
          The right;
       Bot all fals indytars,
       Quest mangers and Iurers,
       And all thise fals out rydars,
          Ar welcom to my sight.

Later, in *The Scourging*, he reveals himself to be a crook and a
shifty rascal—the personification of all the evil antagonism to
Jesus.

Pilatus: In bradyng of batels I am the most bold,
       Therfor my name to you will I dyscry,
         No mys.
       I am full of sotelty,
       ffalshed, gyll, and trechery;
       Therfore am I namyd by clergy
         As mali actoris.

       ffor like as on both sydys the Iren the hamer makith playn,
         So do I, that the law has here in my kepyng;
       The right side to socoure, certys, I am full bayn,
         If I may get therby a vantege or wynyng;
       Then to the fals parte I turne me agayn,
         ffor I se more Vayll will to me be risyng;

This dramatic opposition of Good and Evil makes it possible
for the moral to be much more clearly delivered in this play
than in its counterparts in the other cycles. Jesus is not given an
opportunity to say more than two lines in his own defence and
the trial is a mockery. In other versions of the trial, there is some

semblance of legal formality, but the Wakefield trial is a parody of justice. The scourging scene is very cruel and the trio of torturers brutal in both act and comment:

primus tortor: Lo! here a crowne of thorne / to perch his brane within,
     Putt on his hede with skorne / and gar thyrll the skyn.

By concentrating the evil in Pilate and the good in Jesus, the Wakefield playwright strikes the tragic note. To the Gospel account he has added a personal knowledge of the vile side of human nature and so made the triumph of Pilate's forces all the more immediate; the entry of this Pilate would indeed have drawn hisses, howls of derision and possibly even missiles from the audience. He was presented in terms which would produce in the audience unremitting contempt for such undisguised malice in a human being entrusted with secular authority. The Wakefield cycle makes more of tyrants and profiteers than any of the others, and Pilate emerges as a type of a particular kind of contemporary oppression, the perversion of the law.

SATIRE AND COMPLAINT

Pilate must have been hated by the crowd even more than the bully Herod; the Slaughter of the Innocents was remote in time from a mediæval audience, but crooked lawyers were not, and the bribery and extortions of judges who used legal methods to oppress the poor for personal profit provided subject-matter for many political satirists, allegorists and sermon-makers during the 13th and 14th centuries. The English Dominican John Bromyard completed a large compilation of mendicant sermons, mainly 13th century. This work, called *Summa Predicantium* (*c.* 1360–8), typifies the kind of searing rhetoric in which contemporary friars indulged and has come to be a source-book for scholars investigating the social climate of the late Middle Ages.

Thomas Brinton, Bishop of Rochester at the time of the Peasants' Revolt, was another reforming voice, whose sermons were shot through with the same spirit of rebellion. He described the feudal magnates as extortioners, destroyers of their tenants, detainers of tithes and oblations, violators of church rights, and always the most unpleasant schemers against the Church.

The preachers were the chief social critics, who, far more than the poets, castigated all oppressors of the people, both high and low. The feudal magnate, the judge and the king were thus the habitual targets of preachers and poets. While they were before the crowd in these roles, individual actors were probably in some danger of suffering personal violence, especially if they played their parts convincingly enough to rouse the emotions of the onlookers to a pitch of fury. Lest this should be thought exaggerated, it should be pointed out that performances of Passion plays in some parts of the world can still touch off impetuous reactions, so that it is difficult to discourage volunteers for scourging and crucifixion in performances of these plays in certain remote regions where the Roman Catholic faith is still as steadfast as it was in mediæval England.

The line between fact and entertainment does not seem to have been easy to draw, and it is hard to imagine the full range of the emotional reactions of an unsophisticated audience living under the shadow of a local tyrant who suddenly appears before them embodied in a Herod or a Pharaoh character, the cause of all their immediate earthly woes. But the sources of the characters themselves are to be found in what contemporary preachers had been offering to their congregations in *sermon-exempla*, not only in church but also almost certainly in pulpits set up in the open air even as the pageants were proceeding. Mediæval drama and mediæval preaching shared a common spirit and both made use of the same material, but with the sermon as prime pattern and source, stimulating and determining the nature of the vernacular plays.

There was thus a well-established tradition of satire and complaint: complaint aimed at social and political corruption, such as bribable judges, unfeeling landlords or dishonest traders, at vicious habits, such as meanness, slandering, sycophancy or habitual lying, at those who in the eyes of the Church were delinquent, overdressed, vain of their personal appearance and over-fond of the tavern, and, more generally, at the Seven Deadly Sins of which Man is guilty.

Eventually, Man will die and be judged, and constant reminders of his moral and physical baseness were thought necessary to urge him to repent before the coming of the grave, corporeal corruption and, at one further remove, the pains of Hell. Chaucer's Poor Parson, preaching about penitence, gives a detailed account of the sins of mankind and his road to repentance through contrition, confession, penance and self-discipline. The miracle cycles, and more directly, the morality play, dramatised aspects of such sermons. These elaborated the kind of fate to which neglect of the spirit would inevitably lead—damnation, of course, in the long run, but often more immediate punishments, such as disease, privation or, as in the case of the Colbek Dancers, an unusual kind of divine vengeance.

The mediæval sermon and the moral play both took the form of allegory—in practice this meant a warning tale following an initial idea. Chaucer develops this method for narrative and satiric purposes in several of his *Tales*, such as *The Pardoner's Prologue and Tale*, in which he explains it with the aid of the text 'radix malorum est cupiditas', *The Monk's Tale*, enjoining man not to 'truste in blind prosperitee', and *The Wife of Bath's Tale*, on a non-religious subject, the domestic rights of wives. The preacher tried to show in an arresting manner how doctrine was to be applied to daily life, and his intention, to touch the individual conscience, was precisely that of the writer of the morality play, wherein the theme of repentance was far more clearly reflected.

6

Morality Plays

Although there is a reference by Wyclif to a Yorkshire dramatisation of the Lord's Prayer and survivals like the fragments of *The Pride of Life*, the earliest complete extant example of the morality play proper is *The Castell of Perseverance*, dated about 1425. The Lord's Prayer play was performed about 1380, and this type of drama existed side by side with the miracle cycles. It evidently appeared quite suddenly, so far as scanty evidence shows, and there are hardly any intermediate plays of the gap-bridging kind so convenient for the literary historian endeavouring to show the process of change. One may indulge in a host of speculations on the reasons for the development of moralities at this time connected with the social controversies of the century. The moral play reflected all these trends, pointing a moral and applying it to human behaviour. It was a sermon cast in dramatic form, in content and intention didactic and in plot allegorical.

Allegory has a long history. It may best be described as a figurative narration or description in which the elements of a story are represented in a disguised form in order to give them greater force or interest. The moral play about the Lord's Prayer arose because the Paternoster was believed to afford aid against the Seven Deadly Sins; the play dramatised the contest within the soul of man waged between these sins and the corresponding Christian virtues. Literary historians have cited the 4th-century *Psychomachia* (*Battle for Mansoul*), by Prudentius, as a forerunner of this kind of allegory. In *Psychomachia*, not a drama but a series of jousts, the Soul is the theatre of action and the Virtues fight with the Vices in a succession of single combats. The Virtues always win and the outcome is not in doubt.

Psychomachia is noted as the first poetical Christian allegory and its theme was much illustrated in early religious art. The early English Paternoster play may have been in the *Psychomachia* tradition.

Prudentius, however, also wrote a second allegorical work called *Hamartigenia* (*The Origin of Sin*), in which the Soul is a fortress, attacked by the Devil with a crowd of Vices who are active tempters and not just passive abstractions. In *Hamartigenia* the Vices win, and the human race is subjugated. This second type of allegory might be more appropriately held up as a model for the English morality play. Combat is not single, but general, and an initial defeat of the Virtues in the mediæval plays is followed by a rallying of forces. In the end, we see the triumph of humanity, a universal symbol representing the typical Christian soul, called 'Humanum genus' or 'Mankind', delivered by repentance from evil.

FEAR OF DEATH

There is a third type, conveniently described as the coming of Death, in which prosperity and defiant security abruptly collapse, Man repents and dies in piety. The dramatic conflict is at first won by the Vices, but the moral lesson brings the central figure within sight of utter destruction before saving him through Christian doctrine. Many religious moral plays in England fall into this category, and because of the power of the symbols of destruction or death, portrayed realistically on the stage, they make their lesson immediately and sometimes harshly felt.

What lesson was this? The answer lies in one of the stock themes of mediæval pulpit oratory—the transitoriness of life and the immediacy of death which makes earthly values ultimately worthless. In a Latin sermon, delivered probably in Worcester about 1400, there are some vernacular verses addressed to a 'Lady Everyman', preached on the canticle text 'I am black, but comely':

> Tell us, O lady *de blacworth*, what worth have worldly glory and the aforesaid vanities, of which men are wont to make boast. Once you were fair in body, gentle of blood, privileged with

honours, abounding in houses and wealth. All these things you possessed, and now of all you can say thus—

Now all men mowe sen be me,
That worldys joy is vanyté.
I was a lady; now am I non.
I hadde worchepes; now it is begon.
I was fayr and gentil both.
Now ich man wyle my body loth.
My frendys, my godes me hav forsake.
To wyrmes mete now am I take.
Of al the world now haf I noȝth
bitt gode dedes that I wrogth
Only tho schuln abyde wit me.
Al other thynges aræ vanyte.

This is precisely the theme of *Everyman*, composed about a century later, and a familiar subject in churches wherein congregations were constantly being reminded of their precarious position on the brink of eternity. In an age of recurrent plagues and ignorance of medicine, from pulpit and from poet they heard of the terrible scourge who comes when least expected:

        . . . as thef
To renne thi lif that is the lef.

A late 15th-century revision appears in Mirk's *Festial*, a funeral sermon rejecting worldly goods, riches, 'worshippe' and 'delites'. Only 'gode werkes' will avail against death. The sermon includes this verse:

O mortall folke you may beholde & se
How I lye here sometyme a mighty knyght
The ende of joye and all prosperyte
Is dethe at last. . . .

and on a mediæval trencher of the period, inscribed with the device of a skull, the diner is enjoined:

Truste not this worlde thou wooeful wighte
But lett thy ende be in thy sighte.

In a play in the N-town cycle, when Herod and his soldiers

are in the midst of riotous festivities, Death enters unannounced, the messenger of God, and without speaking dominates the scene—the attention of the audience is riveted on him to the exclusion of all else. Characteristically, he is a robed skeleton, ill-drawn in stained-glass and woodcuts with bones anatomically incorrect. He is not a noble or angelic figure as in earlier religious art but instead a personification of the individual horror of the body's destruction. Meditations on this go back to the 10th-century *Blickling Homilies*, whose author describes corporeal putrefaction and vermiculation with obvious relish:

> ... Their bodies shall lie in the earth and shall be turned to dust, and the flesh shall putrefy and swarm with wormes, and they will flow down over it, and crawl out from all the joints, and nothing else shall live there.

Such pictures become increasingly common, and the vision of Man as 'worm's food' is recurrent. The late-mediæval poet Skelton combines the twin horrors of ossification and fleshly decay:

> Deth holow eyed
> With synnews wyderéd
> With bonys shyderéd
> With his worm etyn maw
> And his gastly jaw. UPON A DEDD MAN'S HEAD

which is much more convincing than the doctrinal message saying that death was but a portal leading through purgatory to a better world. Since redemption was thought to come only at the end of a long period of purgatory the thoughts of a man contemplating death ought to be thoughts of how his sufferings might be lessened. However, the desire to terrify by means of graphic illustrations of the body's fate seems to have led many a narrator away from his doctrinal purpose; the skeleton figure appearing on the stage therefore conjured up a whole host of powerful associations for the mediæval audience which for us are relatively weak. Darkness, pain, burial, decay, bones and Hell's torments gave dimension to the unknown, and when the playwright introduced Death he summed up in a stock figure centuries of admonitory preaching.

There were, of course, some obvious differences between the moralities and the miracle plays. The latter did stress moral truths besides teaching the facts of the Bible, but on the whole did not lend themselves to allegorical formulation except when there was no well-defined Bible story to be followed, as for example in *Antichrist*, or the life of Mary Magdalen before she was converted. The miracle play was collective and yielded its full meaning only when taken in its cycle; it dealt with what were believed to be historical events and its main characters were for the most part ready-made for the playwright by Scripture and inherited tradition. The morality, on the other hand, stood by itself, unconnected to a cycle, and the plots were extremely stereotyped. They afforded less scope for original creation than those of the miracles, which were crowded with major and minor characters, Herod, Pilate, Pharaoh, Noah's wife, Satan, Adam and Eve, Tutivillus, Brewbarret, the shepherds Mak and Gil, and a host of others, both scriptural and non-scriptural. Morality play characters like the Seven Deadly Sins offered limited opportunities for development. Gluttony could hardly be other than a fat lout, Sloth a half-awake lounger, Luxury an overdressed woman, Avarice a grasping old man and Anger continually in a rage.

Morality play personages were always personified vices and virtues, contending for mastery, producing a conflict of sorts and providing material for a plot. The Christian Virtues, the Seven Deadly Sins, Pride of Life, World, Flesh, Mankind, Youth, Age, Holy Church, Riches, Poverty, Wealth and Health, Learning and any social institution, relation or distinction necessary to the didactic aim of the author could be included, and made to behave as though they were human, but always contained within their own narrow definition. By what they said and did, the moral truth which was the subject of the plot was made clear, but since they were not characters but walking abstractions the playwright could not develop them much.

Nevertheless, these personages had in them the seeds of change, and the morality marks a well-defined movement towards the completely secular drama in England. What had been a religious aim gave way to a didactic aim free from theological purpose, so that a message such as 'learning is valuable' could be communicated dramatically. After this, something approaching realistic satire of everyday life developed, and the fact that abstractions could not be endowed with motives for their deeds made it inevitable that a playwright should wish to create real-life characters, with a mixture of good and bad qualities. As the blatant didacticism of the early morality receded, the stage was peopled with human beings, depicting nature's infinite variety, and by this the transition from mediæval to modern drama may be seen.

'THE CASTELL OF PERSEVERANCE'

We have said that the earliest complete morality is *The Castell of Perseverance*. Its stagecraft was not unlike that of the N-town cycle, with a central fixed stage and a number of scaffolds surrounding it; it is thought that *The Castell* also originated in Lincolnshire. The manuscript begins with a drawing of how it was intended to be played. The castle stood in the middle of 'the place', a circular area surrounded by a ditch filled with water or some other barrier, thought by Richard Southern in *Medieval Theatre in the Round* to have been a device for obstructing the view of non-paying spectators. Outside 'the place' were five scaffolds, named for Flesh, World, Belial, Covetousness and God, described in the drawing as 'Sowth, Caro skaffold, West, Mundus skaffold, North, Belial skaffold, North East Covetyse skaffold, Est, deus skaffold'.

There are some quaint-sounding stage directions inscribed on the plan, for example, the rather puzzling

> He that shall play Belial, look that he have gunpowder burning in pipes in his hands and in his ears and in his arse when he goeth to battle . . .

and another showing the influence of colour-symbolism, evident also in tournament and pageant:

> The four daughters shall be clad in mantles, Mercy in white, Righteousness in red altogether, Truth in sad green and Peace in black and they shall play in the place all together till they bring up the soul.

The castle, apparently erected on stilts, is a symbol of security. In contemporary sermons it was a much-used figure of great flexibility, sometimes made to represent God's fortress, sometimes the Devil's. Its obvious source is the feudal tower or fort of which scores were built for defence purposes in the century following the Conquest, and we find references to it from St. Anselm to John Bunyan, though of course Prudentius used it in his *Hamartigenia*, with the Roman fort as his model.

A full account of *The Castell of Perseverance* would take up a good deal of space, for the play is long (3,600 lines) and, like the cycles, tried to picture Man's life from birth to death as it was subject to the conflict between good and evil. 'Perseverance' is a kind of fortitude, 'a vertue that establysheth and confermeth the courage by a perfeccyon of vertues that is in a man', to quote from the 15th-century *Kalender of Shepherdes*. Chaucer's Dame Constance in *The Man of Law's Tale* was endowed with this virtue, but Humanum Genus, the hero of the play, lacks a strong defence against Covetousness. By Confession and Penitence he is led to the castle where he is defended by various Virtues against the attacks of Vices; he then leaves the castle, meets Death, loses his possessions and dies. His Soul appears, reproaches the Body, is conducted to Hell, appeals to Mercy, has the appeal heard before God's judgment-seat and is saved on the basis of Christ's atonement. The play ends with a warning and a *Te Deum*.

The Castell of Perseverance has unity, and its reliance upon colour-symbolism and processional pageantry makes it attractive to the eye; a recent revival showed that it is playable, with a good deal of action distributed between the various scaffolds. The Deadly Sins attack, led by Belial, under a banner displayed by Pride. Flesh is mounted and Gluttony carries a lance. The Virtues use roses as their weapons and rout the Vices with this flower which signifies the Passion.

> I am al beten blak & blo
> with a rose þat on rode was rent . . .

howls Wrath after his defeat in single combat. The moral purpose of the play is dominated by a desire to attack Covetousness, which has an importance bestowed on him equal to that of the Devil and the Flesh. Theologically, Covetousness implied a turning-away from God by concentration on material things—a Deadly Sin of particular concern to contemporary satirists. Chaucer's Pardoner made it the subject of all his sermons. *The Castell of Perseverance* is a powerful play; its major defect is that there is no real comic element, although some of the Vices, like Backbiter and Folly, have humorous possibilities. Inevitably, most of the moralities erred in this direction.

The Castell of Perseverance is one of three plays in a manuscript once owned by an 18th-century antiquary named Cox Macro. The other two, *Wisdom, Who is Christ*, or *Mind, Will, and Understanding*, dated about 1460, and *Mankind*, about 1470, are also heavily theological in content and symbolism. They differ from *The Castell* in that mercy is dispensed in this world and not at God's judgment-seat. *Wisdom* was aimed at an audience of monks and is really a dramatised theological disputation, enlivened by dumb shows and sumptuous costuming, on the relative virtues of the *vita contemplativa*, the ascetic cloistered life of the monastery, and the *vita activa* which took the monk out into the world. A compromise between the two is used by Lucifer to tempt Mind, Will and Understanding into pride, lechery and covetousness. *Mankind*, the last of the Macro plays, is more worldly and the common mediæval symbol of honest toil in the fields, employed by Langland in *Piers Plowman*, permits a greater humanity to enter the drama. It is more interesting dramatically than *Wisdom*, since there are several humorous scenes, touched off by a demon called Tutivillus who appears in the Wakefield play of the Judgment. The play ends with a stock sermon on contempt for the world which is a mere changeable vanity, to be cast out of the mind.

The unreliability of the world is the theme of *Everyman*, the greatest of the English moralities, written about 1500, and possibly based on a Dutch original called *Elkerlijk*. In the Prologue we find *Everyman* described as

> a treatyse how ye hye fader of heven sendeth dethe to somon every creature to come and gyve a counte of theyr lyves in this worlde and is in maner of a morall playe.

Everyman himself is largely an abstraction, concentrating a number of human beings of a specific type into one *persona*. He is the carrier of a warning, reinforced by a stimulus to repentance. The play in which he appears is a sermon-play inculcating the sacramental teaching of the Church, as in the three Macro plays, but with an austere precision and brevity.

As a sacrament involves a priest, the playwright emphasises how essential priesthood is, since in the end Everyman confesses to the priest and is saved. We are not, of course, witnessing a tragedy, for Everyman's death is inevitable, his fear of it universal and, although he has a veneer of humanity imposed upon him by what the dramatist makes him say, his problem is solved not by the vicissitudes of fortune or by any ennobling decision on his part, but by Catholic doctrine. In the hands of Shakespeare, Everyman's heroism would have been determined by the manner of his dying; in the morality play, he goes submissively to his grave, without struggling, but with Truth revealed to him. The Doctor points the moral of the preceding action in a final speech—to forsake Pride, not to trust Beauty, Five-Wits, Strength and Discretion who abandon Man at his ending, and to remember that only Good Deeds will go with him to the grave. The Virtues upon whom he depends are subject to change and for the mediæval theologian change was a mark of the presence of evil. Man is at the last on his own, without Mercy or Pity and

> If his rekenynge be not clere when he doth come,
> God wyll saye *Ite maledicti in ignem eternum* . . .

that is, a text from *Matthew* consigning the cursed into fire everlasting because they have failed to confess a mortal sin. But there is an alternative, expressed in the lines

> . . . he that hath his accounte hole and sounde
> Hye in heven he shall be crounde.

Everyman shows one marked advance in character-drawing; that is, the change in the attitudes of the central personage as the action proceeds and his superficial companions desert him one by one. When Fellowship refuses to go with him he is disappointed and remarks on the old saw:

> . . . in prosperyte men frends may fynde
> Whiche in adversyte be full unkynde . . .

but is not unduly alarmed. The departure of Kindred and Cousin, standing for relatives and friends, is disillusioning to him but still he does no more than remonstrate mildly. Goods refuses to accompany him and admits with complete cynicism that he is a thief of the soul and that as soon as Everyman is dead, he, Goods, will go and deceive someone else. At this barefaced betrayal Everyman suffers a loss of composure and reviles Goods, cursing him as a traitor to God and a trap for men.

Good Deeds then addresses him from the ground, paralysed by Everyman's sins. This inability to move sums up a theological lesson, namely, that even one unrepentant mortal sin on the soul means damnation no matter how many good deeds one may have performed. However, there is divine mercy which has to be taken into account before assuming damnation. In this case the reckoning of Everyman's good deeds is faintly inscribed and difficult to read, but Good Deeds says that he will bring his sister Knowledge to help him give an account of himself before the judgment seat. Knowledge, that is, knowledge that one is in a state of mortal sin, takes Everyman to Confession and he expresses contrition, asks for redemption, receives the sacrament and extreme unction. Beauty, Strength, Discretion and Five-

Wits come to be Everyman's counsellors and all swear to stay with him until he has reached the end of his journey, but when they reach the grave, they abandon him, one by one. Only Good Deeds remains to emphasise the moral:

> All erthly thynges is but vanyte,
> Beaute, Strength and Dyscrecyon do man forsake,
> Folysshe frendes and kynnes men that fayre spake,
> All fleeth save Good Dedes, and that am I.

Everyman is now stripped of everything material and lets out an anguished cry:

> Have mercy on me, God moost myghty,
> And stande by me, thou modor and mayde, holy Mary.

and with Goods Deeds' final ministrations, he commends his soul to God, sinks into his grave and disappears from sight.

The action of this drama is strictly controlled by doctrine. The mediæval Catholic was taught, in works like *De Contemptu Mundi*, that this life was important only in so far as it prepared him for the real life in the next world. The theme that the transitory life on earth was no more than a vestibule to life eternal was a common one and poets harped upon it, echoing contemporary sermons which preached that the world was a testing-time, and governed the nature of one's ultimate reward. Social or material advantages, which were perishable, had no value so far as the final judgment was concerned.

This is a play of which the success depends more on the actors and on the ingenuity of the producer than on the text itself, which needs to be brought strongly to life in words and action. There is scope for clowning in the characters of Goods and Cousin, for subtler satiric humour in Beauty and for sinister posturing by Death. Everyman himself is a part which could make a heavy demand on a good actor. Unimaginatively declaimed, it is liable to drop into woodenness and poker-faced recital. A considerable range of facial expressions and a shrewd understanding of the details of the theme are needed if the changes in Everyman's attitude are to be marked clearly by the actor for the audience to discern. The witty facetious Everyman whom we first meet is dismayed when he begins to realise his position, but he is as yet very far from losing confidence in the things of this world. However, as he goes through a succession of meetings with the allegorical figures representing his social companions, his family, his material possessions and his physical and mental qualities, he sees their promises to him being broken one by one. He is gradually stripped and left naked. All possibilities have gone save the grave, and what Catholic Christian doctrine offers by way of salvation through Good Deeds. As soon as he scourges himself, Everyman's Good Deeds, hitherto bound fast, rises from the ground, saying:

> I thank God, now I can walke and go
> And am delyvered of my sickness and woe . . .

and Knowledge chimes in:

> Now Everyman, be merry and glad!
> Your Good Dedes cometh now; ye may not be sad.
> Now is your Good Dedes hole and sounde,
> Goyng upryght upon the ground.

Doctrinally, this is the turning-point of Everyman's career, when he is first given hope of salvation and, dramatically, it is the real climax of the play, for Everyman now has all the support he can possibly have. The rest of the action is symbolic of Catholic teaching and, after he is dead, Knowledge tells the audience that the human race must all go through the same ordeal. Angel weds Knowledge and takes her to Heaven on account of her 'singular virtue', a common mediæval metaphor expressing the soul's union with God; Angel exhorts all to live well before Doomsday and so achieve this union.

Everyman has an austere power and, having no scene divisions, holds the audience continuously from start to finish. Attention to costume-symbolism and elementary sound effects linked to certain regular incidents, such as the appearance of black-clad Death heralded by the rattle of a tambourine, could, even in broad daylight, awe a superstitious spectator. The play represents a strong development in the form and content of moral plays but at the same time it owes much to the ritualistic character of liturgical drama and to various pageant-plays, which it echoes. There is something of the archetype about *Everyman*; its theme, without doctrinal explanations, has been adapted by several modern playwrights. But although *Everyman* appeals to modern audiences, it is not a modern play; it tells of no doubts or conflict. No struggle is possible against Death and the play's didactic intention is limited to showing sinners how they may repent and be saved, so that Death may be regarded as no more than a passing phase in Man's journey. *Everyman* is perhaps the most undiluted English example of drama as homily. At the same time the line

> O deth, thou comest whan I had thee leest in mynde!

though it sums up the message of centuries of admonitory preaching, is universal and belongs to all ages.

'EVERYMAN', 'DR. FAUSTUS' AND 'HAMLET'

Everyman enacts the mediæval conflict between flesh and spirit as taught by theologians. Its remoteness is obvious when we compare it with Marlowe's *Dr. Faustus*. Marlowe's dramatisation of the conflict clothes the old morality with a fresh humanity. The setting is domestic and the dilemma rests in the mind of Faustus as much as in the external pressures put upon him by Mephistopheles. Like *Tamburlaine*, this is a play of talk, and Marlowe imposed a structural pattern on it by creating a poetic pattern—what in the first chapter of this book we described as poetic drama. Despite the supernatural element involving the pact with the Devil, and the appearance of the Seven Deadly Sins, *Dr. Faustus* is a human play and not heavily moral like *Everyman*, though it inculcates an almost identical lesson involving God's mercy.

But there are important differences. Faustus is a young man, and in the Renaissance view, which is more or less our own view, he is, like all healthy young men, on the side of the bad angel. Mephistopheles represents the natural ideal, the sensual ambitions of youth, which the Renaissance man thought of as the true good—the antithesis of all that mediæval theologians held to be worthy—enthusiasm for beauty, adventure, risk, and an irreverent rejection of tradition and conformity to doctrine such as a play like *Everyman* prescribed. Faustus is a martyr to the swashbuckling virtues, and because he preserves a mediæval consciousness of sin this drama is to be read as an allegorical commentary on the plight of the young intellectual who has to think for himself without the aid of a priest and confessor. Faustus is in fact a crude Hamlet, whom we admire for his intellectual enthusiasm—he asserts all the things which Everyman denies and pulls against mediæval asceticism and its theologically-inspired notions of what constituted vice. The Devil becomes versatile and is an attractive figure, symbolising Man's challenge to explore the unknown and the forbidden. Faustus symbolises the dilemma of his time, for by 1590 the physical world had yielded many of its secrets; a philosophy of art focusing attention on material beauties had grown up, and the Reformation, by banishing the priest as an intermediary between God and Man, had left Man with his problems on his own conscience. Hamlet is the type-figure of the Reformation thinker whose questions remain unanswered, but Faustus at the last is drawn back to the securer Middle Ages and goes to Hell screaming for divine mercy. For Everyman, death is the beginning of a new life; for Faustus it is the end of everything worldly for which he once traded his immortal soul; but for Hamlet it leads to 'The undiscover'd country from whose bourn / No traveller returns': perhaps a better place, perhaps a worse.

END OF RELIGIOUS DRAMA

Moralities in the older tradition of *Everyman* were played less and less often as time went on because they no longer answered the questions which were being asked by educated people. Shakespeare and his contemporaries caught popular interest by reflecting the dilemma of the times, that is to say, the tensions between ethical standards inherited from the Graeco-Roman philosophers, human social relations, and the relations of Man with God. During the period 1450–1600 a confused attitude to religious and secular affairs grew up, theological and political problems developed separate methods of solution, and the older asceticism lost its power over the popular mind. Under Henry VIII the old-established monastic communities, which, working through the cathedral chapters and the parishes, had supported the miracle cycles, were dissolved and their powers dissipated.

Elizabethan drama was closely linked with secularisation. By the early 17th century, contempt for the world had become unfashionable and, except by minority groups, rarely held. The Englishman was well on the way to developing a faith in the facts of science which has since become as naïve as his abandoned belief in the reality of Heaven and Hell. In the name of changing religious doctrine the miracle plays were banned, but in fact politics were the chief determining factor in their rejection by the new Church. They were thought to represent a survival of Roman, that is, foreign cultural domination, as distinct from the moralities, which were accepted as being of domestic origin not linked with any obviously popish doctrines.

Pressure to stop performing the cycles may be traced from the 1530s, when Henry VIII took the first steps to control them, until the 1570s when the four main cycles ran their final courses. Other cycles, now lost, were performed in a modified form until the last decade of Elizabeth's reign but it can be said that the year 1575 saw the end of an era. The Reformation affected every country in Europe, and the forces that ended the religious drama in England were equally hostile to it in France, Germany and Italy. Even in countries which continued to be Catholic, ecclesiastical authorities suppressed the plays, and in Spain alone was there an understandable rejuvenation of the religious stage, which continued until the 18th century. In other European countries, even those less radically affected by Protestant incursions, sacred plays were not performed after the mid-16th century. In England the Corpus Christi procession ceased with them. Its final celebration in York was in 1584.

The miracle cycles were thus hurried out of existence when they were still at the height of their achievement as drama. The municipalities which supported the cycles held out during the reigns of Henry VIII and Edward VI but had to give in to the doctrinal attacks of Archbishop Grindal of York who had 'idolatrous' and 'superstitious' plays stopped in both York and Chester and censored the texts. The people of these cities still wanted to see the old dramas which, after all, were wedded to a tradition over two centuries old and, in spite of their Romish connections, were not to be easily cast aside. Contemporary documents make it quite clear that the four great cycles were ended by authoritarian action at a time when they were still full of vitality and beloved by the townsmen. It is not true to say, as some historians have done, that they ran down through lack of popular or financial support or because secular plays superseded them. Had there been a less oppressive Reformation in England it is likely that the cycles would have continued to thrive for many more years. As it was, the emotional vacuum left by the vanished religious stage was not properly filled. The momentum of the religious dramatic tradition soon exhausted itself so that once the 17th century had passed its first quarter and performances of miracle cycles had receded beyond the extent of human memory, no theological motive survived which was strong enough to encourage even a half-hearted revival. It is this which makes the miracle play difficult to resuscitate.

OBSTACLES TO OUR APPRECIATION

Unlike moralities, which can be performed in modern dress, or Elizabethan drama which can be played in terms of the society that first inspired it, miracle plays may only be 'reconstructed'. A miracle play is a challenge to a modern producer to see what he can do to make his audience perceive the power of the original emotions, the clarity of the didactic dramatisation and the extent to which the old playwright has mastered the material with which he worked. But the faith and joy which were the essence of mediæval idealism have faded, and the conventional manifestations of the Gospel narratives are no longer able to bear the weight of meaning which the miracle playwrights wished to convey to their unlettered audiences. These cycles are very far removed from contemporary notions of what is important, for they cannot be seen as history or as a psychological truth in old-fashioned dress, but rather as museum pieces appealing to what seminal motives of pageantry, hearkening after an antique past, or pockets of unsophisticated humour still remain in our highly-disciplined consciousnesses. Our world has rejected mediæval conceptions of Heaven and Hell, and in any case no miracle play of the Judgment could describe the torments of the damned in language graphic enough to exceed the reality administered with bureaucratic efficiency by the German SS *Einsatzgruppen* from 1941 to 1945. An audience which has survived Hitler and can visualise the effects of an atomic explosion is not going to be easily upset by comic devils or by a sulphurous hell-mouth. Tamburlaine's ranting threats of genocide have been coldly demonstrated in reality, and although Hamlet's puzzle is still our puzzle, neither Faustus nor Everyman speaks directly to a modern audience.

The separation of the modern from the mediæval world has made the early English drama remote, and not even 'a willing suspension of disbelief' can change this, for what is lacking is not an act of imagination but a fact of faith in the kind of truth which miracles and moralities sought to present. These plays were designed for actors and audiences, not for students in studies, and what post-war reviewers have had to say about 'live' performances is therefore extremely valuable as a revelation of what any modern reconstructions, however well done, must lack. They do not yield up any mediæval mystery. What comes down the centuries is as insubstantial as an echo.

7

Interludes

About the beginning of the 16th century the word 'interlude' started entering the titles of plays. Although used long before Chaucer's time to describe a dramatic performance, as in Mannyng's *Handlyng Synne* when the writer admonishes those who indulge in 'entyrludes or syngyng' in the church or church-yard, the word as the historian of drama understands it usually refers to a short moral play in dialogue requiring two or more performers. The sheep-stealing episode in the *Second Shepherds' Play* is one kind of interlude in the sense of 'free insertion', but we are concerned now with interludes that stand by themselves, such as *The Goodly Interlude of Nature*, *An Interlude of Wealth and Health, very Merry and Full of Pastime*, *A Proper New Interlude of the World and the Child*, and others, like *Lusty Iuventus* and *Hyckescorner*, which do not include the word in the title. *Everyman* has all the characteristics of an interlude, and it is not easy to draw the line between the interlude and the earlier morality.

What distinguishes the interludes? First, they were generally shorter than moralities, needed fewer stage accessories and could be acted anywhere at any season in the halls of colleges or in private residences, in roofless theatres or open-air enclosures.

Second, they needed much smaller casts, as few as five men and a boy who took women's parts; each actor played several parts. This meant that only a small stage was required. Account books of Henry VII's reign show that these plays cost about a tenth of what a miracle play or ceremonial disguising did, for the costumes were not elaborate and there were fewer stage properties. The rise of travelling companies meant that economies had to be practised, for playwrights worked to make money and to please patrons and wider audiences. The entertainment motive was stronger in interludes than in the older and more heavily-didactic morality.

Third, interludes did not deal with the whole of Man's life but only with part of it—the sins of youth, the value of learning, the folly of riches, the vanity of the world, the coming of death—all serious subjects but occasionally enlivened by the Vice, depicted in the garb of the domestic fool, portrayed as a slapstick comedian.

Fourth, they preserved mediæval conventions in acting and stage technique but in other respects signalled a departure from mediæval playwriting. After the Reformation divided Europe into a plurality of religious communities there was no longer a characteristically mediæval way of looking at things. England, by virtue of her geographical position, displayed an increased insularity both in religion and politics. She was acutely sensitive to influences from other countries and quick to take a stand against any force thought to threaten absorption into a larger Church or State. All these were human concerns which could not be resolved by reference to revealed religion, and the dramatists found it highly lucrative to write plays reflecting self-conscious patriotism in such a way as to please the ruling class. As early as 1520 the subject-matter of drama had become predominantly secular.

Religious separation was balanced by a re-assertion of the vanishing sense of cultural community with Europe brought about by the aristocracy who looked upon a year or two in Italy or France as an essential conclusion to a gentleman's education. Many plays were written by young men from Oxford and Cambridge who made a studied approach to *avant-garde* tastes by writing in more sophisticated styles, particularly those of Latin or Italian authors, and by trying out experiments with new stage techniques, acting methods, dramatic forms, metrical patterns, and, most significant of all, with the English language, then developing fast.

Broadly speaking, there were three main types of interlude, divided according to subject-matter: the nominally Christian and moral play, the avowedly political play and the patriotically intellectual play. A fourth type, the farcical play, could be added, but the element of naïve fun is present in all three others and in any case there are few purely humorous plays. Of course, none of these types is itself 'pure' and almost any single play of the period will be found to reflect all three tendencies, with one dominant.

SKELTON'S 'MAGNYFYCENCE'

An excellent example is *Magnyfycence, a Goodly Interlude and a Merry, devysed and made by Mayster J. Skelton, poet laureate, late deceasyd*, printed about 1530 but composed several years earlier. It is substantially a morality, in allegorical pattern not unlike *The Castell of Perseverance* and dealing with a political subject from a Christian point of view. Professor Ian Gordon described it as 'the earliest example in English of any dramatic form used for political satire and propaganda'. In fact the earlier *Mankind* has a stronger claim, but Skelton's play is certainly the first to satirise the particular follies of a particular court.

The allegory shows how Magnyfycence, the typical Prince, probably a combination of Skelton's old pupil Henry VIII and Cardinal Wolsey, comes to grief through a succession of bad counsellors and is brought to the brink of suicide before attaining salvation through repentance. Most of the allegorical figures are real or at least recognisable types, but the play ought to be construed in general as much as in particular terms, even though the rapid and ruthless advance of Wolsey under Henry VIII was too good a subject for a satirist like Skelton to miss. Magnyfycence is a fortunate prince, gifted with wealth and the aristocratic capacity to handle it with greatness of spirit and under the noble rule of moderation.

In his *Nicomachean Ethics* Aristotle observed in the course of his essay on Magnificence that 'the Magnificent man is like a man of skill because he can see what is fitting, and can spend largely in good taste'. He is endowed with a virtue which has wealth for its object, so that Magnificence means fitting expense on a large scale, the liberality of great men. Chaucer refers to it in his *Parson's Tale* as 'when a man dooth and perfourmeth grete werkes of goodnesse that he hath begonne'.

Skelton's character therefore starts off almost as an embodiment of virtue, which according to Aristotle had its origin in reason. On the principle of cause and effect, therefore, non-reasonable conduct brings retribution.

This is what happens to Magnyfycence. The drama depicts a fall from prosperity to adversity, the essential requirement of mediæval tragedy. It is not the world of the Christian stoic-ascetic despising worldly prosperity, nor is it that of Everyman realising in the face of death that all is but vanity. There is no conflict, and the issues are pre-decided according to the Graeco-Christian ethics which the author, a Renaissance cleric, seeks to apply to political action. The central character is wooden, without human interest, being simply a prop for his creator's theories. He is not a hero and his actions are not significant because we cannot put ourselves in his place; the didacticism and head-in-air theorism of contemporary writers on statecraft loom large in the play.

Dramatic tension is lacking, but *Magnyfycence* is spectacular and anticipates *King Lear* in the contrast between the luxury of the opening scenes and the fall of the prince, when he has lost his former riches and is reduced to dependence on a few basic moral habits like Perseverance, Circumspection and Good Hope. Lear, however, becomes a hero in his adversity, whereas Magnyfycence is saved by his own repentance and willingness to listen to Redress. The play in its turn is saved mainly by the comic elements, the body of Court Vices headed by Fancy or Wanton Excess and including villains like Counterfeit Countenance, Crafty Conveyance, Cloaked Collusion and Courtly Abusion, who plot against the prince. Here is Cloaked Collusion introducing himself:

> Two faces in a hode couertly I bere
>> Water in the one hande and fyre in the other
> I can fede forth a fole and lede hym by the eyre
>> Falshode-in-felowshyp is my sworne brother.

STAGE II, 11, 710–16

and Courtly Abusion speaking alone:

> What nowe? Let se
> Who loketh on me
> Well rounde aboute,
> Howe gay and how stout
> That I can were
> Courtly my gere: . . .   STAGE II, *14*, 829–34

Magnyfycence, at the height of his peerless ambition, tells us that no prince bears comparison with him:

> Syrus, that soleme syar of Babylon
>   That Israell releysed of theyr captyuyte
> For al his pompe, for all his ryall trone,
>   He may not be comparyd vnto me.
> I am the dyamounde dowtlesse of dygnyte
> Surely it is I that all may saue and spyll
> No man so hardy to worke agaynst my Wyll.

STAGE III, 23, 1473–9

Expressed in high rhetoric and short choppy phrases, studded with picturesque oaths, and cast in eight distinct metres to distinguish varying modes of speech, *Magnyfycence* is technically impressive as a vehicle for the kind of linguistic experimentation with which Skelton is associated.

The character Adversity, an allegorical presentation of Christian Divine Retribution, or the Greek Nemesis, who threatens errant Mankind, eventually attacks Magnyfycence, and strips him of his goods and clothing. Adversity is a solider version of the Death who comes for Everyman.

Magnyfycence deserves what he gets, but there is an additional element in his fate, that of ill-luck. Skelton introduces a sudden change in that Fortune whose fickleness the prince had scorned. The moral ending is conventional, bidding the audience to reject the world, though it has little to do with the main action of the drama which is doctrinaire and based on Aristotelian logic. In its first modern revival at the Canonbury Theatre in 1963 *Magnyfycence* seemed surprisingly fresh. These allegories are, after all, based on fundamental human traits and give an imaginative producer an opportunity to outline the basic facts of our society and its intimate human relationships. Its didacticism prevents *Magnyfycence* from being tragic, but its action comes closer to tragedy than any other drama written in England up to that time.

LYNDSAY'S 'THRIE ESTAITIS'

Another play which fuses political theory with Christian ethics is by far the most brilliantly-written drama of the period. It is not English, but Scots—the only complete example of the mediæval Scots drama. Sir David Lyndsay's *Ane Satyre of the Thrie Estaitis* was written in the early 1530s. Lyndsay was a courtier, diplomat and social-religious reformer, best understood now as a late mediæval Shaw, demanding social justice. 'Satyre' is used in the title of this play in its original sense of *satura*, a mixture in which anything may be found, with a suggestion of the rudeness and crudeness of the satyr.

The aim of the play is to urge reform of Church and State at the expense of corrupt clergy and rapacious nobility and to the advantage of the Commons, who are personified by John the Commonweal, a descendant of Piers Plowman and a symbol of honest toil. Lyndsay wrote to be appreciated by an audience of honest toilers and the play is punctuated by topical allusions. The play is lengthy and is divided into a succession of episodes, referred to loosely as 'interludes' by a contemporary editor who included a number of them in a manuscript anthology.

Ane Satyre falls into two actions. The first is a scene in the Parliament of the Three Estates and is about the reform of the individual ruler, while the second deals with the restoration of the realm to political health. The first is subdivided into five humorous episodes. The mainstay of the action is the fall of the great man whose evil deeds bring down God's discipline—much the same as in *Magnyfycence*. Rex Humanitas is a figure in some respects like Magnyfycence but rather corrupted by Wantones, Sensualitie, Flatterie, Falset and Dissait; reduced to a life of self-indulgence, he is saved by Divine Correction, who states the obvious moral.

The second part is more interesting, being full of fierce satirical comedy; the various vices are depicted in all their inglorious rumbustious vigour before Divine Correction puts them down. Theft, Falset and Dissait are hanged, protesting to the last. Listen to Dissait's last quip as the rope is being placed round his neck:

Second Sergeant:	Now in this halter slip thy heid
	Stand still, me think ȝe draw aback
Dissait:	Allace, maister ȝe hurt my crag
Second Sergeant:	It will hurt better I woid an plak
	Richt now quhen ȝe hing on ane knag 4029–33

Falset is hoisted up complaining of corrupt judges, lawyers and officials and makes a last speech denouncing the priesthood:

> ȝe maryit men evin ȝe luife ȝour lyfis,
> Let never preists be hamilie with ȝour wyfis.
> My wyfe with preists sho doith me greet onricht
> And maid me nine tymes cuckald on ane nicht,
> Fairweil for I am to the widdie wend,
> For quhy Falset maid never ane better end.   4236–41

and the stage directions tell us that

> *Heir sal he be heisit up, and not his figure, and an Craw or ane Ke salbe Castin up as it war his saull.*

The crow symbolised predatoriness and deceit.

Lyndsay makes use of many mediæval literary devices and topical interests to strengthen the framework of his play—the dream convention, the May-morning walk, catalogues of proper names, figures like the Pauper and the Pardoner, the latter sitting with his relics, astrology (James V's hobby), and complaints against familiar abuses, ecclesiastical immorality, the exacting of tithes, neglect of responsibilities, dishonesty and ignorance. In some respects it recalls the earthy mockery of Adam de la Halle's play *Le Jeu d'Adam* (pages 42-3), but its ultimate ancestor is probably Aristophanes.

From stage directions, it seems that *Ane Satyre* was played almost 'in the round'. The spectators were cut off from the performers by a narrow stream which could be crossed easily as the action demanded it. A section of a field was fenced off to form a stage, and there was a gate for players to enter. On the other side of the gate was a pavilion which served as a dressing room, a gallows and the stocks to which the virtues Veritie and Chastity were condemned. Later the tables were turned and Oppressioun, Falset and Dissait took their places. Inside the gate, in the field itself, stood a scaffold, on which Rex Humanitas had his throne. This scaffold also served as a pulpit for the preaching of Veritie, Folly and the Doctor and as a speaking-platform for the Herald, Diligence. The Estates Spiritual and Temporal were provided with seats near the scaffold and there were other seats arranged nearby. Drinking scenes took place at a table.

One of the best exchanges is that in which the Pauper and the Pardoner discuss the price of the latter's pardon.

Pauper: My haly father, quhat wil that pardon cost?
Pardoner: Let se quhat mony thou bearest in thy bag
Pauper: I have ane grot heir bund into ane rag
Pardoner: Hes thou na vther silver bot ane groat?
Pauper: Gif I have mair sir cum and rype my coat
Pardoner: Gif me that grot man, if thou hest na mair
Pauper: With all my heart maister, lo take it thair
           Now let me se ȝour pardon with ȝour leif
Pardoner: Ane thousand ȝeir of pardons I the geif
Pauper: Ane thousand ȝeir? I will not liue sa lang
           Delyuer me it maister and let me gang.   2237–47

The Pauper is not satisfied with the pardon and sees only that he has given up his groat for nothing tangible. He asks for his money back, whereupon the Pardoner explains how his pardon gives him remission in Purgatory. However, the Pauper persists, saying,

    Sall I get nathing for my grot quhill than?

and eventually the argument ends in a fight, with the Pardoner's relics in the stream.

The stage directions were evidently designed to suit the performance at Cupar, Fife, on Whit Tuesday of 1552, and the geographical features mentioned do indeed apply to the Castle Hill in Cupar, mentioned in the Banns or Proclamation as the site of the 1552 performance. *Ane Satyre* was played again in August 1554, before the Queen Regent, but the next recorded performance was at the first Edinburgh Festival in August 1948. It remains as one of the star turns every time it is revived. In the modern performance the costuming is strikingly elaborate and the pageantry and heraldic symbolism make a brilliant spectacle. Although the obvious comparison is with *Magnyfycence*, Lyndsay's play is dramatically far superior to Skelton's and, examined after the passing of four centuries, far less of a curiosity. Like many mediæval poets, Lyndsay disclaims the title of poet and calls his own writing 'ragged rurall vers', but technically he is far ahead of his time in reproducing convincing conversation and making propaganda for the forces of reform, which in the Scotland of that time was desperately needed.

OTHER INTERLUDES

An earlier English play, *The Nature of the Four Elements*, published and probably written by John Rastell in 1517, is an example of the manner in which some writers of interludes handled contemporary interests by the methods of religious dramatists. Influenced by Henry Medwall's *Goodly Interlude of Nature*, Rastell's play, unfortunately incomplete, extols education, reflects current geographical and cosmographical interests and attitudes to the 'new science' of the Renaissance. It opens with a Prologue, spoken by a Messenger, complaining about the shortage of learned books in England and in the English language.

Then the play itself begins. Humanity, a child, son of Natura Naturata, is being taught by Studious Desire, but Sensual Appetite interrupts the educational process to take the pupil to the tavern, a familiar symbol of seaminess in the moral plays. We are not, unfortunately, taken into the tavern itself, and the playwright misses his opportunity of creating a lively scene. The same omission is evident in Medwall's *Nature*, when Sensuality invites Man to a tavern off stage. Nevertheless, there are several comic episodes in *The Four Elements*, marked by the boastful observations of Ignorance, the sum of all the Vices, a familiar figure in interludes. There is a mock geography lesson with a globe depicting America and stressing the dilatoriness of English compared with Spanish, Portuguese and French exploration. In a tub-thumping nationalistic spirit, we are told how much better it would have been had these nations been civilised and converted to religion by the English.

John Redford's *The Play of Wit and Science*, composed about 1535, is a later example of an interlude used as a vehicle for discussing popular interests. In it Ignorance tries to learn from his mother Idleness how to pronounce his own name. The dialogue is not at all sophisticated but, well rehearsed by talented comedians, could be quite funny. John Heywood's *The Four PP—a newe and very mery interlude of a Palmer, Pardoner, Pothecary and Pedlar*, written about 1540, is a non-didactic comic play, having Chaucerian qualities, about a competition to see which of the four men can tell the biggest lie. The characters reveal themselves in dialogue, like Chaucer's pilgrims, and the Palmer wins by declaring that he had never seen a woman lose patience. This may not strike us as being very funny but the original audiences were not so blasé and probably 'rolled in the aisles' at the stock figure of the shrewish wife.

By this time the drama had become a maid-of-all-work. Almost any subject could be dealt with in the form of a play. The Seven Deadly Sins changed their names, first to those of secular abstractions, like Worldly Policy, Private Wealth, Usurped Power, Sedition and other representations of social and political concern, then to those of actual personages. Bishop Bale's *King John*, dated 1557, was the first historical play in English to mingle abstractions with men from real life, and we see on the stage King John, Stephen Langton and the Pope, as well as Nobility, Clergy, Sedition and others from the same family of abstractions. Discussions of sovereignty were prominent during the Tudor period, and there was a good deal of talk about the place of King and Parliament and the legal limitations of royal power, so that the harmony of the commonwealth could be assured by reason. *Respublica*, written in 1553, and described as 'A Merry Interlude', is in the tradition of *Magnyfycence* and *Ane Satyre* and refers closely to the political situation at the time, when Queen Mary had just succeeded to the throne, as the anonymous author tells us in his Prologue, to reform the abuses and ills of the country. In the play she is Nemesis, sent by God. Respublica, a widow, has had ill luck, and in her first appearance makes the familiar complaint about the instability of earthly fortunes and the decay of mortal cities and empires. She does not, however, blame this entirely on Fortune's wheel, saying that good government can be achieved. The rest of the action concerns her quest for this ideal. In the end the enemies of the commonwealth are arrested by Justice and punished by Nemesis.

Sometimes there is a conventional Christian moral conclusion quite unconnected with the matter of the play itself. In *A Newe Interlude of Impacyente Poverte*, printed in 1560, Prosperity loses two thousand pounds to Colhazard gambling in the tavern and is changed into the figure of Poverty, who holds up his own conduct as a fearful example. Unable to bribe the Summoner, Poverty has to do penance, asks for death and is told by Peace that he has been fairly punished. Poverty repents, is given a new garment and turns into Prosperity once again, well on the way to riches, presumably wiser and not subject to the sins of Envy and Misrule which hindered worldly success. Then comes the concluding message, spoken by Peace, enjoining the audience to reject the world and repent because their destiny, even for the gayest of them, is to become 'wyrmes mete'.

This is precisely the moral of *Everyman*. *Impacyente Poverte* is an example of what the moral interlude became immediately before the transition to Elizabethan tragedy: crude, lacking in human interest and confused as to values, for its real moral is that good men become rich. The long exhortations and the serious tone of the drama suggest, however, that the anonymous author's intentions, at least, were religious.

Elizabethan drama could not have sprung directly out of such plays as these, which were simply modifications of the old morality. The greater strength of the English stage in Shakespeare's time had another source in addition to those which we have discussed: the next chapter will deal with this.

8

The Classical Tradition in England

In Chapter 3 we referred to the remnants of classical dramatic tradition in the Middle Ages, pointing out how little direct or traceable influence it had. In England, the classical theatre remained in a state of suspended animation until the Renaissance movement reached the universities. College societies indulged in 'mummings' and 'disguisings' handed down from much earlier times, such as the vesting of the Boy Bishop, the Christmas Lord of Misrule and the Feast of Fools (page 104). These ceremonies may have originated in the mocking of Christian sacraments by actors because of the closing of the Roman theatres, and had a long life, until the 16th century in England and longer still in France.

Account books of the period c. 1480–1550 show that payments were made to strolling players and musicians. One set of Oxford accounts refers to *ludi* and *interludi* but eventually the terms *tragedia* and *comedia* supersede, which probably marks a transition from native morality to formal classical play. By the middle of the 16th century Greek and Latin drama was well established in both Oxford and Cambridge though, since there is no record of a Greek play being acted in Greek, one must presume that the spoken medium was Latin. This in itself kept it out of the hands of popularisers.

The classical Renaissance touched English drama in a number of ways. Nicholas Udall's *Ralph Roister Doister* (1533) is an example of a classically-inspired comedy, constructed according to the principles of Latin drama which, in its original form, attempted to present Romans with the acted drama of the Greek educated classes but in the Romans' own language. We know eleven Roman comedians by name, but only two by their works. These are Plautus and Terence.

PLAUTUS AND TERENCE

Plautus (c. 254–184 B.C.) left twenty *fabulae palliatae*, all freely adapted from Greek New Comedy. Unlike their Greek models, Roman comedies did not have a unifying chorus but were divided into five acts. The commentating function of the chorus was replaced by the 'soliloquy' or by moralising reflections spoken by individual characters. Their similarity to Greek comedies lay in their delineation of stock characters of the lower or middle classes, like the boaster, the scrounger, the slave-dealer, the irascible old gentleman or the cuckolded husband. Most of these plays have a main plot and a sub-plot, and the usual pattern is one of complication, conflict of interests and a happy ending in spite of the preceding network of intrigues. Plautus's *Menaechmi*, for example, depends on the confusion of twins and mistaken identity, and suggested Shakespeare's *Comedy of Errors*. In fact, many of Shakespeare's lighter plays look back to Roman models of impersonation and discovery, confusion of identities and stock situations.

Terence (c. 195–c. 159 B.C.) left only six comedies, also *palliatae*, founded on Greek originals and less freely adapted than those imitated by Plautus. Terence was more refined than Plautus, who was a rollicking poet of the people, and his plots were more decorous and technically more polished. Terence employed blank verse and displayed great metrical variety depending upon a constant exchange of rhythms to reflect transitions of the most delicate kind, but his methods of plot arrangement are similar to those of Plautus. His *Phormio* is a comedy of complex intrigues engineered by Phormio, an unscrupulous parasite who manipulates the law to serve his own ends. It was the model for the first comedy to be written in English prose, George Gascoigne's *Supposes* (1566), and also, in the following century, for Molière's *Les Fourberies de Scapin*. The principal motive of nearly all these plays is love, or rather 'intrigues of the heart', though love scenes as we know them did not occur. Typical of the *palliatae* are plots about the restoration of the foundling to his rightful social heritage, or about the maiden kidnapped and sold into slavery but later rescued by the hero.

There was not much profundity in character delineation, for both Greek and Roman audiences were familiar with the stock figures. These were taken over by the Tudor playwrights, who added a few of their own invention, such as the lawyer, doctor, pedant, astrologer and others from the learned professions of the Renaissance. In this way Greek and Roman drama became a formal standard for Shakespeare's precursors and the ultimate source of the comedy of manners based on 'humours', that is to say, on emphasis of the salient traits of human nature broadened and stressed in stock characters. We associate it chiefly with Ben Jonson, and in a modified form it survives in stage comedy to this day.

'RALPH ROISTER DOISTER'

Ralph Roister Doister is about a hero, Ralph, who is superficially a familiar character out of Plautus, the *miles gloriosus* or swaggering soldier of fortune who reaches his dramatic peak with Bobadil in Jonson's *Every Man in His Humour*. Udall's play, like its Roman prototype, has a Prologue, which maintains the ostensible moral motive of the *palliatae* and claims that this is an interlude against 'the vain-glorious'. However, his conversation with his smooth henchman, Merrygreek, the parasite and professional diner-out, links Ralph not so much with Plautus as with the older English convention of stage conversation, well developed in the miracle cycles.

This late mediæval influence soon comes to dominate the entire play, so that very little of the formal classical pattern survives Udall's handling other than the skeletal plot and the elementary character-sketches of a few male personages. The heroine, Dame Custance, is faithful, honest and of impeccable moral standards, that is to say, in every respect a contrast to Ralph himself. Her nurse, Madge Mumblecrust, and her maids, Tibet Talkapace and Annot Alyface, are English types.

It is a useful and instructive exercise to try and separate the various elements according to character and incident into Graeco-Roman, mediæval, romantic and popular English. The spirit animating the play is English; it was written by a head-master of Eton for his pupils to act. It thus lacks subtlety, sophistication, or embarrassing love tendernesses likely to repel adolescents. On the other hand, it does have an excess of knock-about movement. Disguise, battle and the misunderstood love-letter all provide naïve and uncomplicated motives to action. There is a mock attack by Ralph and his band on Dame Custance's house which reminds us of the St. George play and a three-sided romantic predicament involving Ralph, Custance and her betrothed, Gawin Goodluck, recalling the stereotyped triangular relationship of the mediæval romance. There are several folk-songs, sung by the maids, and a good deal of witty repartee, e.g.

Roister: I would fain kiss you too, good maiden, if I might.
Talkapace: What should that need?
Roister: But to honour you, by this light! I use to kiss all them that
          I love, to God I vow!
Talkapace: Yea, sir? I pray you, when did you last kiss your cow?
Roister: Ye might be proud to kiss me, if ye were wise.
Talkapace: What promotion were therein?

I, 3

and when Ralph is discussing Dame Custance with Merrygreek, and telling him he means to marry her:

Roister: I am utterly dead unless I have my desire.
Merrygreek: Where be the bellows that blew this sudden fire?
Roister: I hear she is worth a thousand pound and more.

I, 2

This comedy is, in itself, not significant but is memorable as an example of what happened to Plautus in English hands and of how his brittle Roman waggishness became transformed by the injection of kindly humour of Chaucerian quality.

'GAMMER GURTON'S NEEDLE'

A superficial reading of the anonymous *Gammer Gurton's Needle*, written by a 'Master of Arts' of Cambridge about 1550, might incline one to conclude its insignificance also, but in fact there is a great deal that repays detailed study in this play. It is certainly much more complicated in origins, form and style than *Ralph Roister Doister*. Formally, it is classical, and adheres to the unities of time and place so that there is no change of scene. The story concerns the loss of a needle by Gammer Gurton. A vagabond, Diccon, the central figure, spreads scandal, and Gammer's neighbour, Dame Chat, is blamed for stealing the needle. Confusions of various kinds hold the stage and eventually the missing instrument is found in the breeches of Gammer's servant, Hodge. The needle device is really too trivial for a modern audience to accept as the motive for so much action, but the play occasionally gets a revival, and at the 1959 Edinburgh Festival the Birmingham Repertory Company demonstrated what could be done with this curious child of a whimsical academic brain. The characters, English rustic types, act and talk in an amusing way, and competent actors in the parts of Diccon, Hodge and Dr. Rat the curate can give the play something of the spirit of the *Second Shepherds' Play*. The types are mostly drawn from the life—the parson, the bailiff, the doctor and the yokels. Diccon, somewhat less real, is a descendant of the comic Vice of the later moralities, with a real love of making mischief without any motive other than that of plunging his village world into chaos. Diccon is a comic Iago, a subtle weaver of webs by hint and innuendo.

The dialect is stage English of the south-west, then as now accepted as 'country-bumpkin' speech:

Hodge: ich know thars not within this land
          A muryner cat then Gyb is, betwixt the Tems and Tyne;
          Shase as much wyt in her head almost as chave in mine.

                                                                III, *4*

and there is a hearty folk-song, 'Back and side go bare', sung by Diccon. In spite of this farmyard atmosphere, *Gammer Gurton's Needle* is not to be dismissed as a grotesque 'remain' of a transitional period. In language, metre, rhyme and alliterative concentration it stands out as a remarkably interesting piece, a repository of archaic forms, coinages, unusual phraseology and living dialect words anticipating Spenser's *Shepheardes Calender*, a much more unblushingly pedantic work which is linguistically in the same category. The meticulous construction of the plot, without superfluity, around a basic absurdity, is the work of a playwright whose technique is clearly modelled upon the Roman comedians, particularly Terence. His nearest relative among known dramatists is Thomas Heywood, for he reproduces the background of Heywood's interludes with equal pungency but imposes the discipline of classical comedy form. In this way he displays a technical grasp quite different from the loose construction which marks the Heywood plays. A good deal of these comic effects depend upon rigidity—the patterned and regularly foolish behaviour of the characters and the predictable slip—and this is much more effectively communicated when the action is meticulously disciplined. The impression made by *Gammer Gurton's Needle* is one of cleverness and learning, and the impression of noisy yokel talk is deliberately misleading. It has certainly deceived many critics into pronouncing a quick dismissal of a play not only interesting to the scholar but also quite actable.

EUROPEAN ROMANTIC INFLUENCE

Another influence on Tudor drama can best be described as 'European' or 'romantic'. The Renaissance brought with it sentimentalism, a contrast to the austerity of late mediæval plays like *Everyman*, and a greater lavishness of scene. Shakespeare's comedies are often given Italian backgrounds—Venice, Verona, Padua, Florence, Naples or Milan—not because the playwright had ever been there and wished to reflect personal experience, but because Italy had long been connected in the popular mind with a freedom and a licence which England lacked, and had a *dolce vita* reputation permitting English dramatic characters to shed their puritanism as though they were Latins. Under sunny Italian skies anything could happen, and English audiences could accept this foreign morality because it did not touch them directly. This Italian influence is indirectly perceptible in English dramatic writing even before 1500 and we have a play by Henry Medwall, *Fulgens and Lucrece*, based on an Italian original, a French rendering of it and an earlier English version. F. S. Boas in his introduction to *Five Pre-Shakespearean Comedies* says that 'the characters are the first, so far as we know, to appear in an English play within a framework that is neither Biblical nor allegorical but purely secular'.

This makes *Fulgens and Lucrece* an important play marking the actual transition but its place in dramatic history is obscure since it was a lost play until 1919. Shakespeare almost certainly knew it, however, for the comic sub-plot, the most interesting feature of the play, bears a strong resemblance to that of *Twelfth Night*. A similar touch of sophistication is perceptible in the anonymous *Calisto and Meliboëa* (1530) which has its source in a long-winded Spanish tragedy called *Celestina*, composed in the Ovidian tradition, but in the hands of the English adapter suffering a sea-change to a happy ending. In both these plays native traits dominate the imported southern European warmth and the introduction of an unfamiliar setting did not alter the essential 'Englishness' of the *dramatis personae*, who, like Chaucer's Greeks, behave like Londoners of the upper-bourgeois class.

SENECA

Greater reference must be made to Seneca (*c.* 4 B.C.–A.D. 65), who exercised a strong influence on the development of Tudor tragedy. Seneca, a rich man who did not write for popular audiences, lived during the decline of the Roman republic. His style is distinguished by a tendency to extravagance, emotional exaggeration and delight in wordiness. Seneca's audiences were probably held captive by the force of his language rather than by the profundity of his statements, perhaps because the era was one of political stagnation so that pictures of violence on the stage made up to some extent for a lack of purpose in real life—a set of circumstances not unfamiliar to us today.

Senecan plays, constructed on Greek models and the only

Roman tragedies extant, were interlogues in a series, separated by music, intended for recitation rather than for the stage proper. They were sometimes delivered in Roman baths to literary cliques who appreciated clever epigrams and rhetorical pedantry. A surfeit of descriptive matter—what we call 'purple patches'— and a poverty-stricken plot embellished by revelations of carnage, bloodthirsty tyrants and physical excesses marked the Senecan tragedy.

Seneca was a Stoic and subscribed to a philosophical view that evil may be got rid of by reasoning, that all is for the best, that we are all part of some ultimately good plan and that Man should therefore be resigned to whatever fate the active life may have in store for him, painful though it might be. This makes tragedy impossible, for tragedy depends on personal suffering. The questions we posed in the first chapter typifying those expressed dramatically in Shakespeare's tragedies could easily be answered by a Stoic. For example, he would say that the gods punish the innocent and aid the guilty because it is in the nature of things that they should do so. The gods made the universe and its laws and they must obey the latter. In his *Agamemnon* Seneca makes his chorus say:

> Fate places us so high, that so
> To surer ruin we may go.
> The meanest things in longest fortune live.
> Then happy he whose modest soul
> In safety seeks a nearer goal.
> Fearing to leave the friendly shore,
> He rows with unambitious oar
> Content in low security to thrive.

reminding us of Sophocles in *Antigone* whose warning words foreshadow the romantic fatalism of the Byronic hero:

> For mortals greatly to wish is greatly to suffer.

The Stoic could afford to neglect material ambition because he scorned poverty, pain and struggle as a way of life. He was able to describe the world's horrors without participating in them, and this is what Senecan tragedy tended to do. Seneca's most obvious influence on English drama was on *Gorboduc* (1557) by Thomas Norton and Thomas Sackville, two Oxford men.

'GORBODUC'

Gorboduc was the first English play to follow the 'rules' of classical drama. Senecan example determined its shape, its division into five acts, the use of a chorus and of a messenger to report action, and the employment of blank verse as a metre fit to express direct speech. Blank verse, that is, unrhymed iambic pentameter, was first used by the Earl of Surrey to represent the Virgilian hexameter, then by Sackville and Norton in *Gorboduc* in imitation of Seneca's iambic verse.

It may be asked why it was that Seneca, a second-rate writer of tragedy, became the chief model for Tudor playwrights and exercised such an influence on Shakespeare and his contemporaries? In the first place, the Tudors were ignorant of Greek. Sophocles and Euripides were known to scholars, but not Aeschylus. The theory and practice of tragedy was based on the works of the only classical writer they knew at first hand, namely, Seneca, supported by the literary precepts of Horace, who occupied a similar position in criticism. Although Aristotle was frequently cited as an authority, the 'rules' associated with his name were those voiced by interpreters of the Italian Renaissance, like Scaliger, Minturno, Robortello and Castelvetro, who cited Seneca as an example of all that was most majestic and perfect in classical tragedians. There were Senecan imitations by Italians, turned into Latin, as early as 1315, and into Italian from 1499 onwards.

These Italian critics believed that tragedy must have an unhappy ending. The Greeks held no such view—Sophocles and Aristotle saw it as dignified in character and serious in theme and language, but the melodramatic character of Elizabethan tragedy and the high-flown eloquence beloved of the Renaissance experimenter in stage speech, which went well with the extravagant actions portrayed or referred to by a Marlowe or a Kyd, were inherited from Senecan models.

Gorboduc was played before Queen Elizabeth in 1561 at the Christmas Revels of the Inner Temple. Its purpose was moral-political, like *Magnyfycence* and *Ane Satyre*, for the authors wished to illustrate for the Queen's benefit the possible plight of England should the succession to her throne not be settled. It was, in fact, a serious attempt to move the Queen and make her marry so as to resolve the succession.

The plot is about the legendary British king, Gorboduc, who divided his kingdom between his sons Ferrex and Porrex. Porrex kills Ferrex; his mother, Queen Videna, kills Porrex and the infuriated populace kills Gorboduc and the Queen. As in *King Lear*, the tragic action stems from the king's ill-considered disposal of his kingdom and the moral lesson is that the causes of suffering are responsible human actions, not the turn of Fortune's wheel. The fact that the characters are human and not abstract personifications helps to make this a clearer statement of human political responsibility than that found in *Respublica*. The two long disquisitions of Arostus and Eubulus in the last act represent the political kernel of the play. The examples are drawn from pseudo-history and the political maxims are presented in an authoritative form, namely, that of Senecan tragedy.

The tragic heroes of the drama are Gorboduc and the suffering State, but although there are many Senecan features, such as the interest in situation, introspective passages, elaborate monologues, neatly-worded sententiousness, reported rather than visible action and much talk of ambition, pride and lust for power, the closest parallel to Sackville and Norton's play is the mediæval morality and not the Senecan fragment *Phoenissae* on which it is directly modelled. The good and evil counsellors that give advice to Gorboduc and his sons are simply dressed-up Virtues and Vices.

More interesting is the verse itself. Much of it is wooden and declamatory but occasionally it shows signs of a vitality indicating that the style and content of dramatic speech was changing. Marcella's description of the death of Porrex, slain by his mother, is poetic drama; the action lurks in the words:

Marcella: But heare hys ruthefull end.
  The noble prince, pearst with the sodeine wound,
  Out of his wretched slumber hastely start,
  Whose strength now fayling straight he ouerthrew,
  When in the fall his eyes euen new vnclosed
  Behelde the Queene, and cryed to her for helpe.
  We then, alas, the ladies which that time
  Did there attend, seeing that heynous deede,
  And hearing him ofte call the wretched name
  Of mother, and to crye to her for aide,
  Whose direfull hand gaue him the mortall wound,
  Pitying (alas) for nought els could we do
  His ruthefull end, ranne to the wofull bedde,
  Dispoyled straight his brest, and all we might
  Wiped in vaine with napkins next at hand,
  The sodeine streames of bloud that flushed fast
  Out of the gaping wound. O what a looke,
  O what a ruthefull stedfast eye me thought
  He fixt vpon my face, which to my death
  Will neuer part fro me, when with a braide
  A deepe fet sigh he gaue, and therewithall
  Clasping his handes, to heauen he cast his sight.
  And straight pale death pressing within his face
  The flying ghost his mortall corpes forsooke.

IV, 2, 203–26

and later, the same speaker's heavily pathetic recollection of the murdered prince:

  Ah noble prince, how oft haue I behelde
  Thee mounted on thy fierce and traumpling stede
  Shining in armour bright before the tilt,
  And with thy mistresse sleue tied on thy helme,
  And charge thy staffe to please thy ladies eye,
  That bowed the head peece of thy frendly foe?
  How oft in armes on horse to bend the mace?
  How oft in armes on foote to breake the sworde,
  Which neuer now these eyes may see againe.

IV, 2, 248–56

This is still a long way from Marlowe, but there is movement and some depth in the bright figures, which, although they may strike us as stereotyped, must have been fresh enough to the original audience. The appeal of this heavily-ornamented rhetoric is direct and unsubtle, but *Gorboduc* is not rich in such passages and there is hardly any psychological connection between these static characters and what they say. The play is a moral play, in the didactic tradition, with its argument supported by a Chorus and dumb shows, but full of affected, turgid writing and pedantic repetition of a few political maxims. Only rarely is there some sign that the authors are struggling to escape from their rhetorical straitjacket.

The Senecan technique, of which the most obvious feature was the set speech, continued to influence English playwrights until the 1590s, but this classical drama was really designed for aristocratic or educated audiences. Plays in the English tradition never wandered far from the popular track and any tendencies to do so were rough-hewn by earthier enthusiasms. At the time *Gorboduc* was first performed indoors, miracle cycles were still being played out in the streets of English towns. Shakespeare was born early enough to be able to look upon religious drama as living drama and to be directly influenced by its ancient and spectacular pageantry. The ritual pattern in individual plays, like *Henry V*, *Twelfth Night*, *Measure For Measure* or *The Winter's Tale* is unmistakable. In *Hamlet* the relations between the Prince and his uncle may be described formally in duelling terms of stroke and counterstroke, an orderly process also apparent in the internal conflicts which underlie their continuous actions. A mediæval sense of ceremony permeates the play.

When the religious drama ended in England, classical and European—particularly Italian—influences had sufficiently blended with mediæval and local traditions to make Elizabethan audiences familiar with the versatility suggested by the repertoire of the Players at the Court of Elsinore, described by Polonius as

The best actors in the world, either for tragedy, comedy, history, pastoral, pastoral-comical, historical-pastoral, tragical-historical, tragical-comical-historical-pastoral, scene individable, or poem unlimited; Seneca cannot be too heavy, nor Plautus too light. For the law of writ and the liberty, these are the only men.

HAMLET, II, 2, 424-30

Bibliography

1. Texts and modernised versions of the plays quoted from or referred to:

Adams, J. Q., ed. *The Chief Pre-Shakespearean Dramas. A Selection of Plays Illustrating the History of the English Drama from its Origin Down to Shakespeare.* (Houghton Mifflin, Boston & New York, 1924.)

Block, K. S., ed. *Ludus Coventriae or the Plaie called Corpus Christi.* (Early English Text Society, 1922.)

Boas, F. S., ed. *Five Pre-Shakespearean Comedies.* (World's Classics, Oxford Univ. Press, 1934.) Contains *Fulgens & Lucrece, The Four PP, Ralph Roister Doister, Gammer Gurton's Needle, Supposes,* with a short introduction.

Bond, R. W., ed. *Early Plays from the Italian.* (Clarendon Press, 1911.) Includes *Supposes* and has a long scholarly introduction.

Cawley, A. C., ed. *Everyman and Mediaeval Miracle Plays.* (Everyman's Library, Dent, 1962.) A useful undergraduate's edition, with simplified text and some running translation provided.

The Wakefield Pageants in the Towneley Cycle. (Manchester Univ. Press, 1958.) Contains a useful bibliography of editions and secondary sources.

Cunliffe, J. W., ed. *Early English Classical Tragedies.* (Clarendon Press, 1912.) Contains *Gorboduc* and has a stimulating and scholarly introductory essay.

Deimling, H. and Matthews, G. W. edd. *The Chester Plays.* (Early English Text Society, Vol. I, 1892, ed. by H. Deimling, Vol. II, 1916, ed. by G. W. Matthews; both reprinted 1959.)

England, G., ed. *The Towneley Plays*. (Early English Text Society, 1897.) Sidenotes and introduction by A. W. Pollard.

Farmer, J. S., ed. Reprints of Early English Drama Society, London, originally published in 1905–7, reprinted 1966 by Charles W. Traylen, Guildford. 5 volumes containing *Mankind, Nature, Hickescorner, Respublica, Impatient Poverty, Calisto & Meliboëa, King John*, etc.

Furnivall, F. J. and Pollard, A. W., edd. *The Macro Plays*. (Early English Text Society, 1904.) Contains *The Castell of Perseverance*, etc.

Greenberg, N., ed. *The Play of Daniel*. (Oxford Univ. Press, 1959.) Text by Rev. R. Weakland, O.S.B. Contains suggestions for amateur performances.

Hussey, M., ed. *The Chester Mystery Plays*. (Heinemann, 1958.) Adapted into modern English with a short introduction.

Kinsley, J., ed. *Ane Satyre of the Thrie Estaitis* (by Sir David Lyndsay). (Cassell, 1954.) Introduction by Agnes Mure Mackenzie.

Manly, J. M., ed. *Specimens of the Pre-Shaksperean Drama*. (Athenaeum Press Series, Ginn. Boston, 1897, 2 vols.)

Pollard, A. W., ed. *English Miracle Plays, Moralities and Interludes*. (Clarendon Press, 8th edition, 1959.) Contains *Everyman* and part of *The Castell of Perseverance*.

Purvis, J. S., ed. *The York Cycle of Mystery Plays* (S.P.C.K., 1957.) In modern English.

Ramsay, R. L., ed. *Magnyfycence* by John Skelton. (Early English Text Society, 1908.) Has a very scholarly preface.

Rose, M., ed. *The Wakefield Mystery Plays*. (Evans Brothers, 1961.) In modern English. Contains a valuable commentary written from the point of view of an imaginative modern producer of the plays.

Studer, P., ed. *Le Mystère d'Adam, an Anglo-Norman Drama of the Twelfth Century*. (Manchester Univ. Press, 1918.)

Thomas, R. G., ed. *Ten Miracle Plays*. (York Medieval Texts Series, Arnold, 1966.) Has a concise bibliography and glossary and a modern introduction designed for undergraduates and the upper forms of schools.

Toulmin-Smith, L., ed. *The York Plays.* (Clarendon Press, 1885: Russell and Russell, New York, 1963.) Prefaced by an extremely interesting introduction based upon research into the York civic records.

Young, K. *The Drama of the Mediæval Church.* (Clarendon Press, 1933, 2 vols.) Contains texts of the liturgical dramas, and is a work of monumental scholarship.

2. Secondary Sources, critical studies, etc.

Anderson, M. D. *Drama and Imagery in English Medieval Churches.* (Cambridge Univ. Press, 1963.)

Boas, F. S. *University Drama in the Tudor Age.* (Clarendon Press, 1914.)

Chambers, E. K. *The English Folk-Play.* (Clarendon Press, 1933.)

The Mediaeval Stage. (Clarendon Press, 1903, 2 vols.)

English Literature at the Close of the Middle Ages. (Clarendon Press, 1947.) Section on mediæval drama.

Craig, H. *English Religious Drama of the Middle Ages.* (Clarendon Press, 1955.)

Donovan, R. B. *The Liturgical Drama in Medieval Spain.* (Pontifical Institute of Mediaeval Studies, Toronto, 1958.) Chapter 2 is a sound general introduction to the study of liturgical plays.

Farnham, W. *The Medieval Heritage of Elizabethan Tragedy,* with bibliographical note. (Blackwell, 1956.)

Frank, G. *The Medieval French Drama.* (Clarendon Press, 1954.) Includes a select bibliography.

Gardiner, H. C. *Mysteries' End. An Investigation of the Last Days of the Medieval Religious Stage.* (Yale Univ. Press, 1946.)

Gayley, C. M. *Plays of our Forefathers.* (Duffield & Co., New York, 1907: Chatto & Windus.)

Hardison, O. B. *Christian Rite and Christian Drama in the Middle Ages; Essays in the Origin and Early History of Modern Drama.* (Johns Hopkins Press, Baltimore, 1965.)

Hughes, Dom Anselm, ed. *Early Medieval Music up to 1300.* (New Oxford History of Music, Oxford Univ. Press, 1954.) Chapter VI on 'Liturgical Drama', by W. L. Smoldon, is a comprehensive account.

Ingram, R. W. 'The Use of Music in English Miracle Plays'. (*Anglia*, LXXV, 55-76, Tübingen, 1957.) Has concise review of selected secondary sources to 1955.

Kolve, V. A. *The Play Called Corpus Christi*. (Arnold, 1966.) Deals with the genre, form and meaning in the plays, and includes an interesting discussion of laughter within mediæval religious contexts. Has a detailed select bibliography.

MacQueen, J. 'Ane Satyre of the Thrie Estaitis'. (*Studies in Scottish Literature*, III, No. 3, January 1966, 129-43.)

Mill, A. J. *Mediaeval Plays in Scotland*. (St. Andrews Univ. Publications, No. 24. Edinburgh and London 1927.)

Morgan, M. '"High Fraud": Paradox and Double-Plot in the English Shepherds' Plays.' (*Speculum*, XXXIX, No. 4, 676-89. October 1964. Cambridge, Massachusetts.)

Owst, G. R. *Literature and Pulpit in Medieval England*. (1st edition, Cambridge Univ. Press, 1933; 2nd edition, Blackwell, 1961.) See especially the chapter on 'Sermon and Drama'.

Prosser, E. *Drama and Religion in the English Mystery Plays: a Re-evaluation*. (Stanford Univ. Press, 1961.) Chapter I surveys the recent history of dramatic criticism of the plays.

Robinson, J. W. 'The Art of the York Realist'. (*Modern Philology*, LX, No. 4, May 1963, 241-51. Chicago Univ. Press.)

Rossiter, A. P. *English Drama from Early Times to the Elizabethans*. (Hutchinson, 1950.)

Salter, F. M. *Medieval Drama in Chester*. (Univ. of Toronto Press, 1955.) An original approach to staging, written for delivery as lectures.

Southern, R. *The Mediaeval Theatre in the Round*. (Faber, 1957.) A study of the staging of *The Castle of Perseverance* and related matters.

Spiers, J. 'The Mystery Cycle: Some Towneley Cycle Plays'. (*Scrutiny*, XVIII, No. 2 and XVIII, No. 4, Autumn 1951 and June 1952, 86-117 and 246-65. Cambridge Univ. Press.) Deals with folk-material in the Christian context of the plays.

Stratman, C. J. *Bibliography of Medieval Drama*. (Univ. of California Press, 1954.) Exhaustive list of primary and secondary sources indispensable to the serious student.

Unwin, G. *The Gilds and Companies of London*. (Allen, 1908, 3rd edition, 1938, Cass, 4th edition, 1963.)

Wickham G. *Early English Stages, 1300 to 1660*, Vol. I, 1300–1576. (Routledge & Kegan Paul, 1959.)

Williams, A. *The Drama of Medieval England*. (Michigan Univ. Press, 1961) with a bibliography.

The Characterisation of Pilate in the Towneley Plays. (Michigan Univ. Press, 1950) with a bibliography.

3. Illustrated works on mediæval religious art:

Clark, J. M. *The Dance of Death by Hans Holbein*. (Phaidon Press, 1947.) Has a short introduction, notes and bibliography of the subject.

Evans, Joan. *The Flowering of the Middle Ages*. (Thames & Hudson, 1966.) Magnificently illustrated introduction to the life and thought of the period. Chapter VI, 'King Death, Morality, Judgment and Remembrance', by T. S. R. Boase, is particularly interesting.

Frankl, Paul. *Gothic Architecture*. (Pelican History of Art, Penguin, 1962.) A standard work, with nearly 200 plates.

Gardner, Arthur. *English Medieval Sculpture*. (Cambridge Univ. Press, 1951.) With 683 photographs and related commentary.

Grigson, Geoffrey. *English Cathedrals*. (Thames & Hudson, 1950.) Has full plates with a foreword by G. G.

Jantzen, Hans. *High Gothic*. (Constable, 1962.) An account of the cathedrals of Chartres, Rheims and Amiens, with photographs.

Lowrie, Walter. *Art in the Early Church*. (Pantheon Books, New York, 1947.) With 153 plates.

Simson, Otto V. *The Gothic Cathedral: the Origins of Gothic Architecture & the Medieval Concept of Order*. (Routledge & Kegan Paul, 1956.) Beautifully illustrated account of Chartres.

Weber, F. P. *Aspects of Death in Art and Epigram. Illustrated Especially by Medals, Engraved Gems, Jewels, Ivories, Antique Pottery, etc.* (T. Fisher Unwin and B. Quaritch, 1914, 2nd edition enlarged.) 123 illustrations. Part IB refers to morality plays.

Index